PERSONAL
BANKRUPTCY

*What Every Debtor and
Creditor Needs to Know*

Practising Law Institute Guides

ESTATE PLANNING
How to Preserve Your Estate for Your Loved Ones
by Jerome A. Manning

INVESTOR'S RIGHTS HANDBOOK
• Stocks • Bonds • Mutual Funds
• Other Securities Investments
by Larry D. Soderquist

YOUR RIGHTS IN THE WORKPLACE
Everything Employees Need to Know
by Henry H. Perritt, Jr.

PERSONAL BANKRUPTCY
What Every Debtor and Creditor Needs to Know
by William C. Hillman

A Practising Law Institute Guide

PERSONAL BANKRUPTCY

*What Every Debtor and
Creditor Needs to Know*

WILLIAM C. HILLMAN

United States Bankruptcy Judge
District of Massachusetts

Practising Law Institute

NEW YORK

Library of Congress Catalog Card Number: 93-85791
ISBN: 0-87224-060-6

Acknowledgements

Primary thanks must go to Attorney Marnie M. Crouch, whose efforts brought order to a somewhat chaotic manuscript, and whose research assistance was most valuable. If any mistakes remain in the text, it is because I wrote something and did not pass it by her.

Judge Joan N. Feeney deserves a special award of merit for volunteering to read the entire manuscript.

As always, The Practising Law Institute's Bill Cubberly provided valuable guidance.

Contents

A N
AUTHENTIC NARRATIVE
O F   T H E
P R O C E E D I N G S
Under a COMMISSION of BANKRUPTCY

A G A I N S T

J O H N   P E R R O T T,

Late of *Ludgate – Hill*, LACEMAN;

Who was executed in SMITHFIELD, on *Wedne/day, November* 11, 1761

For CONCEALING his EFFECTS,

Including every Tranfaction from the awarding the Commiffion, to the Time of his Condemnation.

Publifhed under the INSPECTION of the

PRINCIPAL ACTING ASSIGNEE.

P A R T   I.

" HEAVEN *may forgive a Crime to* Penitence ;
" *For* Heaven *can judge if,* Penitence *be* true :
" *But,* MAN, *who knows not Hearts, mu/t make* Examples ;
" *Which like a Warning-piece mu/t be /hot off,*
" *To fright the* reft *from* Crimes.————
DRYDEN.

L O N D O N :
Printed for R. GRIFFITHS in the *Strand.*
M.DCC.LXI.

[Price ONE SHILLING.]

The early bankruptcy laws in England were very harsh. Concealing assets might be punishable by death, as this title from a 1761 book shows.

PART

1

What This Book Is About

You probably picked up this book for one of three reasons:

- you find yourself in financial difficulties right now;
- you have guaranteed debts of, or co-signed loans for, someone who is having financial problems; or
- someone with financial problems owes *you* money.

In all three cases you want to know something about the bankruptcy laws. Under most circumstances, the bankruptcy laws of the United States will provide the best solution for a debtor and, less often, for a creditor or guarantor. However, the laws are complicated, not only in the way they are written, but in the way they are applied by judges.

This book is an explanation of the bankruptcy laws, and how they affect debtors and creditors. No one should file a bankruptcy petition without understanding where that event can lead. This book will help you make an informed decision about a bankruptcy filing and its consequences.

What is this book NOT about?

Except in passing, this book does not cover business reorganizations, which are the subject of Chapter 11 of the Bankruptcy Code, or bankruptcy proceedings involving partnerships. Those subjects are extremely complicated and beyond the scope of this text.

Although much of the information in this book would apply to a liquidation proceeding for a business corporation under Chapter 7 of the Bankruptcy Code, the book's primary focus is on people: individuals or couples who are involved in bankruptcy proceedings under Chapter 7 or Chapter 13.

Do I have to read the whole book?

As you go through the early chapters you'll learn what later material applies to you. You can then review only the relevant parts.

Start with part 2: How the Bankruptcy Law Works. It will give you an idea of where you will want to turn next. Part 3 will help you to work out your present financial condition. If you already know where you stand financially, you may want to go directly to part 5 (Eligibility) and then to part 6 (Chapter 7) or part 7 (Chapter 13). Those parts will direct you to other portions of the book that can address particular problems that you have.

What if I'm a creditor?

The early chapters of the book will give you an overview of the bankruptcy process. Part 14 is especially designed to give creditors the information that they need to exercise their rights.

I guaranteed or co-signed the debt of someone who has filed bankruptcy; where should I look?

You'll want to read part 15 to see how your rights are affected if the person for whom you signed files for protection under the Bankruptcy Code. If you are being asked to act as a co-signer or guarantor, you may want to read that part before you sign.

Is bankruptcy the sole remedy for money problems?

Bankruptcy can be very helpful to some people with financial problems, but for others it can increase their difficulties. As you read or browse through the material that follows, you may find that certain parts of the bankruptcy laws would make filing a petition a bad idea for you, or that your situation should be disclosed to and discussed with a bankruptcy attorney before making a final decision.

For example, assume John and Mary Doe have a home, two cars, lots of debts, and insufficient income to pay all of their creditors in full and on time. Depending upon how they got into their present situation, and where they are going in the future, a trip to the Bankruptcy Court may have any of these consequences:

- They keep their home and cars, subject to the mortgage and auto loans, and walk away from all their other debts.
- They lose their home and cars and start out broke, but out of debt.
- They keep their home, cars, and related loans and agree to pay a portion of their other debts over three years.

- They are denied a discharge of their debts by the Bankruptcy Court, leaving them worse off than ever before, still owing everything and possibly facing criminal charges because of the way they handled their assets.

What this book is about is whether any of these scenarios is in your future.

Read on!

PART

2

How the Bankruptcy Law Works

Before there was any bankruptcy system, there was no way for a person to escape liability for debts. People unable to pay their bills were often sent to debtors' prisons. Failure to pay a debt was a crime. Even the early bankruptcy laws in England were still very harsh (for example, concealing assets might be punishable by death).

What is the main purpose of the bankruptcy laws?

To paraphrase the Supreme Court of the United States, a major purpose of the bankruptcy laws is to give the honest but unfortunate debtor a new opportunity in life and a clear field for future effort, unhampered by the pressure and discouragement of preexisting debt. More briefly, the goal of the Bankruptcy Code is a fresh start for deserving debtors.

Where does bankruptcy law come from?

In the United States, it's mainly a federal question; Congress enacts laws on bankruptcy. There has been a bankruptcy law continuously in force since 1898. In a few states there are "debtor relief" statutes that may provide help for financially troubled individuals, but the state laws lack the national scope and power to alter contracts and other financial relationships that the Bankruptcy Code possesses.

Just what is this "Bankruptcy Code" you're talking about?

The current version of the bankruptcy laws, called the Bankruptcy Code, was enacted in 1978, although it has been amended in various ways almost every year since then. It creates a comprehensive system of adjusting the relationships between a person and that person's creditors.

The Bankruptcy Code is title 11 of the United States Code (the federal statutes are collected under fifty topics, called titles). The legal reference to a section of the Bankruptcy Code is "11 U.S.C." followed by a section number. So, section 341 is referred to as "11 U.S.C. § 341."

I keep reading about "going into Chapter 11"; what's a chapter?

Chapter 11 is one of the divisions in *title* 11. (You may have noticed that what would be chapters in most books are called parts here; we wanted to avoid confusion with the Chapters of the Code.) Within the Code there are a number of different procedures, commonly known by the number of the chapter in which the operative provisions appear:

Chapter 7 deals with liquidations. Basically, all of the property of a debtor, less certain exempt property, is divided among the creditors according to their priorities.

Chapter 13 covers individual reorganization plans. It provides a way for a person with a regular income and limited amounts of debt to pay off creditors with regular payments over three to five years.

Chapter 11 is for reorganizations. It is used primarily for businesses, but it is available to individuals. It will not be discussed in detail in this book.

Chapter 12 is for farmers. It is discussed very briefly in this book. Added in 1986, it is a new chapter and requires the attention of an attorney familiar with its provisions. A section at the end of part 5 explains the qualifications for using Chapter 12.

Are there any other sources of bankruptcy law?

In addition to the Bankruptcy Code, procedure in the bankruptcy court is governed by the Federal Rules of Bankruptcy Procedure (FRBP). The FRBP, together with local rules of the individual courts, specify procedures for commencing bankruptcy cases, filing claims, selling property, and many other matters that arise in a bankruptcy case.

What are some of the terms bankruptcy practitioners use?

There is a detailed glossary of bankruptcy terms at the back of the book, but, for immediate use, here is a basic introduction to the specialized words most often used in bankruptcy cases:

The person who files a bankruptcy petition (in a voluntary case) or against whom one is filed by creditors (an involuntary case) is called the "**debtor**." The term "bankrupt" is no longer used in this way. The case is named after the debtor. For example, "*In re John Jones, Debtor*" is the title (also called a case name or caption) of John's bankruptcy proceedings. ("*In re*" is the most common indication that a lawsuit is "in regard to" someone or something; "In the Matter of" is also often seen.) If a husband and wife file a joint petition, the title would be "*In re John Jones and Mary Jones, Debtors*." For some purposes in the bankruptcy forms, the first-named person is called the "debtor" and the other is called the "spouse."

The property of the debtor handled within the bankruptcy proceeding is called the "**estate**." There are frequently disputes about whether certain assets are "property of the estate," or somehow exempted or excluded from the estate. You will learn more about that later in this book.

The persons charged with either handling or overseeing property of the estate are "**trustees**." There are two kinds of trustees. The "trustee in bankruptcy," commonly called just the "trustee," is named to be in charge of a particular Chapter 7 or Chapter 13 case. In a Chapter 7 case, he or she gathers the assets, makes distributions to creditors, and performs other functions regarding the estate. Chapter 13 trustees perform more limited duties. We will discuss many of those tasks later.

In Chapter 7 cases, the trustee will be named from a panel of trustees that probably has many members, who are generally either lawyers or accountants. In Chapter 13 cases, there is generally only one person, or only a few persons, who handle all Chapter 13 cases in a particular court.

The trustee in bankruptcy is appointed by the **"United States Trustee,"** who is another type of trustee altogether. The United States Trustee is an officer of the United States Department of Justice. His or her designated representatives in each bankruptcy court monitor the entire bankruptcy process, seeing to it that all of the parties to the case do what they are supposed to do. If someone fails to perform his or her duties -- for example, a debtor fails to file reports as required -- the United States Trustee may file a motion to dismiss the case. If a debtor is in a proceeding under Chapter 13 and is not performing under the proposed plan, the Chapter 13 trustee at the behest of the United States Trustee may file a motion to convert the case to Chapter 7 for liquidation or to dismiss it altogether. (In a few states, the duties of the United States Trustee are performed in part by the bankruptcy judge and in part by a court officer called the Bankruptcy Administrator.)

In this book, "trustee" will always mean the Chapter 7 or Chapter 13 trustee in bankruptcy. When we mean the United States Trustee we'll say so.

The **"bankruptcy judge,"** of course, presides over all cases. Generally speaking, though, the judge does not become involved in particular cases, unless there are disputes that require judicial rulings, or fees are being sought by a trustee or a professional (lawyer, accountant, auctioneer, etc.) retained by the trustee or debtor. Certain preliminary hearings, including the meeting of creditors that is held in every case, are handled by the trustee or a representative of the United States Trustee.

What is the Bankruptcy Court?

Technically, the Bankruptcy Court is part of the United States district court for the district where it is located. The Bankruptcy Court has its own printed forms, its own courtrooms, its own clerk of court and staff, and, most important, its own judges.

Some bankruptcy judges do not wear robes in court but that does not affect their authority. They are still called "Your Honor," and treated with respect.

How are cases assigned to judges?

In bankruptcy courts with more than one judge, cases are generally assigned to a particular judge at the time the first papers are filed. There is no choice; assignments are made in strict rotation. The initials of the judge will normally follow the case number. For example, Case No. 92-1234- JQA is probably being handled by a judge whose initials are JQA. In most courts, the designated judge will handle all proceedings in the case requiring action by a judge. If your case is very simple, you may never see the judge at all.

Where are bankruptcy cases filed?

Bankruptcy cases are generally filed in the court that covers the area where the person filing has lived for the 180 days before the petition is filed. If a person has lived in more than one place during that time, then the proper place is where the person spent more of that period than any other place, even if it is not the person's current residence.

What protection do I have upon the filing of the bankruptcy petition?

In all bankruptcy cases, the so-called automatic stay arises immediately upon the filing of the petition. It protects the debtor from any attempt to collect claims that arose prior to the commencement of the bankruptcy case. It also stops new legal actions against the debtor, and halts all pending cases against the debtor. It also prevents pre-filing creditors from attaching or garnishing the debtor's assets. In a Chapter 13 case, but not in a case under Chapter 7, the stay gives some protection to a guarantor or co-signer of the debtor's obligations. (The automatic stay is discussed in more detail in the parts of this book that follow.)

A QUICK TOUR THROUGH CHAPTER 7

The details of Chapter 7 are given in much more detail in what follows, but these are the basic steps in the process:

1. Debtor files the original petition and pays a $120 fee plus a new $30 administrative fee.
2. Debtor files schedules A through J (they're included in the forms at the back of the book), which contain lists of all assets, debts, exemptions claimed, and other such matters.

3. If appropriate, the debtor files a statement of intentions regarding certain consumer debts and applications to reaffirm certain debts and redeem certain property.
4. At the section 341 meeting, also called the first meeting of creditors, the debtor answers questions asked by the trustee and creditors under oath.
5. Debtor turns over to the trustee books and records and all property of the estate.
6. If appropriate, the debtor files to avoid liens that impair exemptions.
7. If appropriate, the court conducts a hearing or trial to determine whether all or certain debts can or cannot be discharged.
8. Debtor receives discharge.

A QUICK TOUR THROUGH CHAPTER 13

The details of Chapter 13 are given in much more detail in what follows, but these are the basic steps in the process:

1. Debtor files the original petition and pays a $120 fee plus the new $30 administrative fee.
2. Debtor files schedules A through J (they're included in the forms at the back of the book), which contain lists of all assets, debts, exemptions claimed, and other such matters.
3. Debtor files statement of affairs and Chapter 13 plan, detailing ability to pay and the terms upon which the debtor proposes to pay creditors.

4. Within thirty days of plan filing, debtor commences making payments.
5. At the section 341 meeting, the debtor answers questions asked by the trustee and creditors.
6. Debtor attends confirmation hearing and obtains order confirming the Chapter 13 plan.
7. Debtor makes all monthly payments required by the plan.
8. Debtor receives discharge.

PART

3

Where Do You Stand?

The purpose of this book is to help you to understand how the bankruptcy system works, and how it can work for you, primarily as a debtor taking advantage of the protection the law affords. It also addresses the concerns of creditors and guarantors in parts 14 and 15, but the emphasis is to educate those who think that they should at least consider the possible relief available under the bankruptcy laws.

Am I insolvent?

Assuming you are in the earliest stages of the decision-making process, this part will help you to find out where you are, so that you can determine where you can go. This requires an understanding of the concept of "insolvency."

Under the Bankruptcy Code, for individuals, "insolvency" means that your liabilities exceed your assets. Outside of the context of bankruptcy, this is called the balance-sheet test: you total up all of your assets, subtract all of your liabilities, and see what is left. If your assets

15

exceed your liabilities, you have a "positive net worth;" if it's the other way around, you have a "negative net worth."

Sit down with your paperwork and the assistance of appendix B to determine your net worth. But that is only the first step.

All right, I have a negative net worth; should I go straight to the courthouse?

Even if you have negative net worth — you owe more money than you have either in cash or from the value of your assets — bankruptcy need not be a consideration. So long as you can meet the required payments on your debts, the value of the underlying collateral is, for the most part, unimportant.

Then why did you ask me to work through appendix B?

You will want to determine your net worth, however, because it may be possible to rearrange assets (sell some, or whatever) and change your entire financial picture. If you do not have a reasonable estimate of your net worth, you should work through appendix B.

What should I do next?

The second step in financial analysis is the preparation of what is called, in the business world, the profit-and-loss statement. The statement compares what is coming in with what is going out. For individuals, the same study is simply a review of income and expenses. You will find excellent forms to help you organize your income and expense information in appendix A — look for Schedules I and J to the petition. (If you *can* pay all of your bills as payments come due, you probably don't need this book. But if your analysis shows that you have a negative cash flow — expenses exceed income — read on.)

When will bankruptcy make sense for me?

Bankruptcy will make sense for you if you need relief from your present obligations, most of your debts are dischargeable, and you will be able to keep property that you really need. That sentence was easy to write, but you'll want to, at least, scan much of the rest of this book to see if your situation fits the necessary pattern. Then it will be time to consult with your bankruptcy attorney.

PART

4

Do You Need
a Lawyer?

Strictly speaking, a person can prepare and file a bankruptcy petition under Chapter 7 or Chapter 13 without any legal help. Some people do it. There are many books on the market that tell you how to complete the forms. You'll see from what follows that it is generally a mistake and a false economy not to use the services of a bankruptcy lawyer.

I'm flat busted and I've done nothing wrong; do I have to pay a lawyer?

If you have no assets at all, except perhaps the clothes on your back, and you haven't done any of the things that might result in a denial of your discharge in bankruptcy or the discharge of a particular debt (as discussed elsewhere in this book), you could probably do it alone.

Aside from that very simple case — and it might not be so simple if you once had assets that you no longer have — the answer to the question is yes, you do need a lawyer. The old saying that people who represent themselves "have a fool for a client" is particularly true in the bankruptcy court.

Is it really that complex?

The bankruptcy laws can be extraordinarily complicated. Many mistakes people make by trying to do it on their own often cannot be corrected later. Even the simplest choices involve uncertainties and risks if you are not thoroughly familiar with the law. For example:

- It is often difficult to determine exactly which exemptions should be selected under state or federal law.
- There are technical time limits during which certain things must be done. Many of the limits cannot be extended; others can be stretched, but only by taking the proper steps at the proper time. If you miss one of the deadlines, you may lose valuable rights.
- The bankruptcy courts used to disagree on whether the funds you have set aside for retirement would be exempt from your bankruptcy, or would be taken from you and divided among your creditors. In early 1992 the question was finally resolved by the United States Supreme Court. However, the application of the exemption requires a particular choice on the bankruptcy forms, and the classification of individual retirement accounts (IRAs) may depend upon an interpretation of a state statute.

- You can sometimes keep a car or other asset by reaffirming the debt. Deciding whether to do so is tricky, and the decision must be made early in the bankruptcy case. Judges differ on what debts they will allow you to reaffirm. A bankruptcy lawyer will know the attitude of the local judges.
- If you have had property attached or seized during the preference period (as explained elsewhere in the book), you may be able to recover the property. To do so requires a special legal proceeding that is beyond the abilities of a nonlawyer.
- If you sold or gave away any property in a way that gives the appearance that you didn't get full value for it, the trustee or creditors may challenge the transfer. You really can't defend that on your own.
- If you want to try to discharge student loans under the "hardship" rule, you'll need a lawyer.
- If you've ever given a personal financial statement or credit information that a creditor claims is false, you'd better have a lawyer to defend you. If not, the debt may be ruled to be nondischargeable and remain alive after bankruptcy.
- Certain kinds of credit card debt incurred shortly before bankruptcy may not be dischargeable. If a creditor raises the issue, you'll need a lawyer to state your case.
- It may be possible to get rid of or reduce certain judicial liens on your home, but you'll need a lawyer to figure out if those provisions apply to you.

What makes someone a "bankruptcy lawyer"?

A bankruptcy lawyer is one who spends a significant amount of his or her practice in the bankruptcy court where you would be filing. The joke is that you need a lawyer "who knows where the courthouse is." You need more than that. You need a lawyer who is up to date on the latest bankruptcy rules and decisions, who knows the local rules (there are different ones in every bankruptcy court, some unwritten), and who knows the attitude of the judges on critical issues.

Where do I find the right lawyer?

It's a bit of a job. If you have a friend who has used a bankruptcy lawyer, ask for an opinion. If you have used a lawyer for other matters, ask him or her if bankruptcy cases are also within his or her expertise. If not, your lawyer may be able to refer you to someone known to be competent in the area. If this fails, try the referral service of the local bar association. It's generally listed under "Lawyer Referral Service" in the Yellow Pages.

Should I check the advertisements in the paper?

Lawyers who advertise that they specialize in bankruptcy matters are of two types, those who are truly expert and those who only claim to be. Like any other important decision, you should investigate beyond just reading an advertisement.

What should I watch out for?

Beware of services that are operated by nonlawyers and claim that they will help you fill out the forms. Also beware of referrals from lenders or creditors; their interests may be sharply different from yours. There are a number of technical issues and judgment calls that can be made only by an experienced professional. The decisions go far beyond filling in the forms.

To repeat: YES, you do need a lawyer in a bankruptcy case.

PART

5

Are You Eligible to File?

Most persons are eligible to file a bankruptcy case. Creditors of a person can file certain types of involuntary petitions against that person, but that is not common. Here are the requirements for eligibility under Chapters 7, 13, and 12 of the Bankruptcy Code.

FILING UNDER CHAPTER 7

Any individual living in the United States can file a voluntary petition for relief under Chapter 7 of the Bankruptcy Code. However, if that person has previously received a bankruptcy discharge in a case started less than seven years before the new case, no discharge can be granted. The practical result is that you should not expect relief in bankruptcy more often than once every seven years.

There are two other exceptions that affect eligibility and involve persons who have been in the bankruptcy court recently. Persons who have had their case dismissed for willfully failing to obey orders of the court or to appear when required to do so or those who have voluntarily dismissed their case when faced with a motion for relief from stay cannot file again until 180 days have passed. Sometimes judges will allow a dismissal by a debtor on condition that the debtor not refile for a year or even longer. There is some question about whether such orders are valid, since the statute only prohibits filing for 180 days. Nevertheless, if a judge enters such an order it would take a major effort to test its correctness.

When a married couple is in financial trouble, it is common for them to file a joint petition. That right is expressly set out in the Bankruptcy Code. Only one filing fee is paid. The cases are usually treated as a single case for all purposes, but that isn't required. It is possible that circumstances may require that the spouses be treated differently.

FILING UNDER CHAPTER 13

A voluntary petition under Chapter 13 can be filed only by a person with a regular income who is able to satisfy the conditions of Chapter 7 and who is not a stockbroker or a commodities broker. This means that the person must have an income that is sufficiently stable and regular to enable him or her to make payments under a Chapter 13 plan. That decision, of course, is affected by the amount of money owed.

To have a "regular income," your income must be *stable*. If you receive Social Security benefits or disability benefits, you may qualify for Chapter 13 protection. If you are self-employed, you may have income stable enough to file a Chapter 13 plan, but you will have to show that your employment provides regular income.

Further, you must owe less than $100,000 in unsecured debts and $350,000 in secured debts that are, in the words of the Bankruptcy Code, "noncontingent and liquidated" at the time you file your petition. If you file a Chapter 13 petition with your spouse, your total indebtedness may not be greater than these limitations. However, if, for example, the mortgage on your house is $375,000, but your house is worth only $300,000, under certain limited circumstances discussed in part 7 you may still be able to take advantage of Chapter 13. It works this way: since your house is worth only $300,000, only that amount is treated as secured debt. What happens to the $75,000 mortgage balance? It is treated as unsecured and goes against the $100,000 maximum for that class of debt.

The same rules with respect to dismissals for refusal to abide by court orders or in response to relief from stay motions apply in Chapter 13.

INVOLUNTARY PETITIONS

Creditors of a person can file a petition against that person only under Chapters 7 and 11 of the Bankruptcy Code. There are no involuntary filings under Chapter 13 or Chapter 12. Since involuntary cases under Chapter 11 against individuals are quite rare, we will not discuss them further.

Involuntary cases normally require the signatures of three creditors with undisputed claims totalling at least $5,000. If there are fewer than twelve creditors, only one creditor has to sign the petition.

We do not expect you to use this book either to bring or to defend an involuntary petition. Both have very substantial risks for the amateur and you would be foolish to undertake either task without experienced and competent counsel. As a result, we'll not discuss those procedures further.

FILING UNDER CHAPTER 12

This book will not cover the new provisions governing the bankruptcy of family farmers. However, if you think that you might qualify under those provisions, you should know the basic tests that must be satisfied. They are set forth in the following paragraphs.

Only a person, corporation, or partnership that meets the definition of a family farmer with a regular annual income can file a petition under Chapter 12. The test for income is similar to that for a Chapter 13 filing. The income must be sufficiently stable and regular to enable the farmer to make payments under a plan.

Joint petitions of a husband and wife are permitted.

A farmer is a person who is engaged in a "farming operation," which is defined in the law as "farming, tillage of the soil, dairy farming, ranching, production or raising of crops, poultry, or livestock, and production of poultry or livestock products in an unmanufactured state."

There are also financial tests to be met, three in the case of an individual or married couple:

1. Total debts cannot exceed $1,500,000.
2. Leaving out any debt not related to farming that is secured by the farmer's principal residence, not less than 80 percent of liquidated, noncontingent debts must arise out of a farming operation owned and operated by the farmer.
3. More than 50 percent of the farmer's income must come from the farming operation.

If the farmer is a corporation or a partnership (other than between husband and wife), the business must satisfy these tests:

1. Total debts cannot exceed $1,500,000.
2. More than 80 percent of its assets must be related to the farming operation.
3. Leaving out any debt not related to farming that is secured by the principal residence of a shareholder or partner, not less than 80 percent of liquidated, non-contingent debts must arise out of the farming operation.
4. More than 50 percent of the stock in the corporation, or partnership interests in the partnership, must be held by one family and their relatives, with "relatives" being determined by a very technical legal rule.

PART

6

How Chapter 7 Works

Once a person has decided that a Chapter 7 filing is both possible (see part 5) and beneficial, the petition must be prepared. The Official Forms should be used. You'll find copies of them at the end of this book, although many attorneys use computer-generated forms that have the same contents.

What goes into my petition?

You'll see that the information required is extremely detailed. You will have most of the financial information ready if you have completed the calculations described in appendix B. It is very important to have all of the information as up-to-date and accurate as possible. Leaving things out, if discovered, can, at a minimum, make people think that you are hiding things, and, at a maximum, be a bankruptcy crime.

I've filled it out; now what do I do?

The petition is filed with the appropriate Bankruptcy Court. The filing fee is currently $120, and it is generally paid at the time of filing. A new $30 administrative fee was added in December 1992.

What if even that amount is too much all at once?

There is a provision in the Bankruptcy Rules for paying the filing fee (but not the administrative fee) in not more than four payments, all within 120 days of the filing. Because the time allowed for payments is so short, most debtors manage to gather the necessary funds to pay in full initially. If installment payments are selected and a payment is missed, most courts automatically dismiss the case.

Is this where the automatic stay comes in?

The filing of the petition automatically creates an injunction, called a "stay." That means that creditors are prohibited from trying to collect debts or to foreclose on property without specific authorization by the Bankruptcy Court.

How important is that stay?

The automatic stay is the primary reason many debtors file for bankruptcy. They believe that the extra time it gives them will allow them to work out their problems with creditors. Many petitions are filed the day before a scheduled auction sale of the debtor's property, or on the eve of an eviction. The stay puts the auction or eviction on hold, until either the creditor receives court permission to proceed or the property is abandoned by the trustee.

Subject to certain exceptions that will be mentioned shortly, the stay is extremely broad. In the words of the statute, it operates as a stay, applicable to all entities, of —

(1) the commencement or continuation, including the issuance or employment of process, of a judicial, administrative, or other action or proceeding against the debtor that was or could have been commenced before the commencement of the case under [the Bankruptcy Code], or to recover a claim against the debtor that arose before the commencement of the case . . .; (2) the enforcement, against the debtor or against property of the estate, of a judgment obtained before the commencement of the case . . .; (3) any act to obtain possession of property of the estate or of property from the estate or to exercise control over property of the estate; (4) any act to create, perfect, or enforce any lien against property of the estate; (5) any act to create, perfect, or enforce against property of the debtor any lien to the extent that such lien secures a claim that arose before the commencement of the case under this title; (6) any act to collect, assess, or recover a claim against the debtor that arose before the commencement of the case . . .; (7) the setoff of any debt owing to the debtor that arose before the commencement of the case . . . against any claim against the debtor; and (8) the commencement or continuation of a proceeding before the United States Tax Court concerning the debtor.

That was fascinating; what do I have to know?

There are sixteen exceptions to the automatic stay listed in the statute. That is, there are sixteen kinds of actions against the debtor that may continue despite the filing of the bankruptcy petition. The exceptions that are most important to individuals include:

1. The commencement or continuation of criminal actions against the debtor.
2. The collection of alimony, maintenance, or support from property that is not property of the estate.
3. The commencement or enforcement of any action by a governmental unit under its so-called police powers, which generally concern public health and safety and environmental and related matters.
4. The issuance of a notice of tax deficiency.
5. If a landlord of *nonresidential* real estate has terminated the lease or other tenancy before the filing of the petition, the landlord may continue to enforce its rights to obtain possession.

Do the courts really use the stay?

Bankruptcy courts are generally quite ready to enforce the stay and levy penalties for contempt of court against those who violate it.

If I were a creditor, would I have any recourse?

Creditors may seek relief from the stay by filing an appropriate motion in the court. A hearing will be held at which the creditor must establish that it should be permitted to proceed. In the usual case, the creditor is a secured creditor who seeks permission to start or continue foreclosure proceedings, or a landlord seeking to evict a tenant.

Does the protection of the automatic stay ever break down?

If the creditor is able to show that the amount of the debt exceeds the value of the property, or that the debtor has continuously been unable or unwilling to make payments even though the amount of the debt is less than the value of the property, it may be difficult for the debtor to resist the motion to lift the stay. Some courts, in Chapter 7 cases, pay little attention to the debtor's objections on the theory that only the Chapter 7 trustee has the power to object (remember that equity in your property belongs to the bankruptcy estate and is administered by the trustee).

Are there any other circumstances?

Abandonment is the reason the automatic stay is not effective in many cases. If the trustee believes that there is no equity in a piece of property for the estate - - that is, that the total of mortgages and other valid liens exceeds the value of the property — the trustee may abandon the property. The reason is simple — no equity in the property means that the trustee would be administering an asset from which the unsecured creditors would recover nothing; it would be a waste of effort.

Once the property is abandoned, the holders of mortgages and other liens are free to proceed. The automatic stay no longer applies.

I'm buying my car on time; is there anything special I have to do?

Where some of the property of the estate consists of consumer goods that are subject to liens, such as household goods or cars purchased on a "time payment" basis, the debtor must file a statement of intention with regard to such property within thirty days of the original filing. Most debtors file the statement with the original petition. Retention of property and reaffirmation of such debts is covered in part 13.

You mentioned the "first meeting of creditors"; what's that all about?

Not long after the petition is filed (although it may be a few months in very busy courts) the debtor will be directed to appear at a meeting called under section 341 of the Bankruptcy Code. This is called a "341 meeting" or the "first meeting of creditors" in bankruptcy jargon.

The debtor must appear at that meeting and "submit to examination under oath." The debtor can be questioned by the trustee, the United States Trustee, or any creditor who is present. All creditors listed in the schedules to the original petition will be notified of the 341 meeting and may attend to find out more about the debtor's circumstances. Sometimes the questioning gets hot and heavy, especially if the debtor is suspected of having concealed or disposed of assets. Typically, the questioning is not intense and the meeting very brief.

Assuming I tell the truth and shame the Devil, is there anything else to be concerned about at the 341 meeting?

Some creditors, especially credit card issuers and large chain stores, regularly send representatives to the 341 meeting. They use the opportunity to talk to the debtor about reaffirming debts. The problems presented by this practice are discussed in part 13.

Do I have to appear at the 341 meeting?

If you do not appear at the 341 meeting, your case will probably be dismissed, and you will have wasted the filing fee, the legal fees, and a lot of effort. If the date that the court sets is not good for you because of your work schedule or for other reasons, it is possible to have it rescheduled. Any rescheduling should be done with the trustee's consent and just as soon as the notice is received. You may have to agree to send a new notice of the 341 meeting to all of your creditors and to extend the deadlines for filing objections to discharge or nondischargeability complaints in order to obtain a new date.

At least I'll have to go through that only once, right?

The section 341 meeting may not be the only time the debtor is required to testify about finances, property, and the like. The Bankruptcy Code permits the meeting to be continued, and it permits creditors to ask for permission to take further testimony from the debtor. Such questioning, called a 2004 examination after the number of the bankruptcy rule, is generally much more detailed than the proceedings at the section 341 meeting. Your lawyer will know what issues will be addressed if you are called for such an examination and can help you prepare for it. The debtor with nothing to hide has nothing to fear.

What happens next?

The United States Trustee will have appointed a trustee for the case. That person is generally an experienced bankruptcy lawyer who serves as trustee in hundreds of cases.

What does a trustee do?

Under the law, the trustee now "owns" all of the debtor's property, and the debtor is theoretically required to surrender all property and all records to the trustee. As a practical matter, little property actually changes hands without a specific request from the trustee to the debtor. The trustee cannot take over the debtor's home in the ordinary case. Some of the trustee's duties are:

- Reviewing the schedules and statements of affairs. If they are not filed on time, the court or the trustee may have the case dismissed.
- Examining the debtor at the section 341 meeting. If the debtor does not appear, the trustee may move to dismiss the case.
- Objecting to the debtor's discharge if that is appropriate, within sixty days of the section 341 meeting (see part 9).
- Objecting to claimed exemptions if that is appropriate, within thirty days of the concluded section 341 meeting (see part 11).

- If there are no assets to administer, abandoning any property; filing a no-asset report; and having the case closed.

- If there are assets, selling or otherwise disposing of them; bringing any appropriate actions to recover fraudulent conveyances or preferences (see part 12); paying creditors according to their statutory priorities; filing a report of receipts and disbursements; and having the case closed.

Is there anything else that may happen?

Once the case is underway, many things may happen. The debtor may attempt to avoid certain liens on property that impair claimed exemptions or for other reasons (see part 13). Creditors may bring proceedings to determine the dischargeability of debts or to obtain a ruling that the debtor should not be discharged at all. These matters are discussed in part 9.

When all matters have been clarified, the assets of the estate are distributed and the case will be closed.

When you say the assets are distributed, what do you mean?

After the payment of secured creditors, assets are sold and the proceeds are generally distributed in this order:

1. Expenses of administration, including professional fees.
2. Certain claims in involuntary cases.
3. Unpaid wages, salaries, and commissions due to employees, to a maximum of $2,000 per individual earned within ninety days of bankruptcy.

4. Contributions to employee benefit plans within specified limits.
5. Certain claims of farmers and fishermen against the debtor, up to $2,000 each.
6. Consumer deposits up to $900 per person.
7. Most unsecured tax claims — state, federal, and local. If there is a tax lien, the claims may not fall into this class.
8. General creditors.

And that's it?

The debtor is discharged from all liabilities not reaffirmed or determined to be nondischargeable. Creditors whose claims have been discharged are forbidden to take any further action against the debtor.

PART

7

How Chapter 13 Works

Note: This part and part 8 deal with individual reorganization plans under Chapter 13 of the Bankruptcy Code, which were formerly known as "wage-earner plans." The information you need to know is set forth as simply as possible, but it is still quite complicated. If you are interested in the possibility of using Chapter 13, scan parts 7 and 8 first, then go back and reread the portions that seem to apply to your situation.

You'll hear that Chapter 13 is so simple that anyone can do it without a lawyer. The information in parts 7 and 8 is *probably the best evidence of why that is not true.*

Who can use Chapter 13?

In part 5, we discussed the qualifications a person or married couple must have to file a petition under Chapter 13. In brief, Chapter 13 is available to persons

- with stable, regular incomes

- who owe less than $100,000 in unsecured debts; and
- who owe less than $350,000 in noncontingent and liquidated secured debts.

What are the basic differences between Chapter 7 and Chapter 13?

Chapter 7 requires you to give up any property you own that is not exempt. The Chapter 7 trustee will sell that property and distribute the money from the sale to your creditors. Your future income is yours. Chapter 13, on the other hand, allows you to keep much or even all of your property and to pay your creditors from your future income under the protection of the Bankruptcy Court. You will be required to prepare a Chapter 13 plan that spells out how you intend to use your income to pay all or a portion of your debts.

Can one of my creditors walk in and make me file a Chapter 13 plan?

Only you can file a Chapter 13 case and plan — no one can force you to file under Chapter 13. In contrast, under certain circumstances, described in parts 5 and 14, creditors can institute involuntary Chapter 7 proceedings.

Aren't there some things common to both Chapter 7 and Chapter 13?

In many respects, filing a Chapter 13 case triggers the same events that were discussed in part 6 of this book (How Chapter 7 Works). For example, filing the petition automatically causes a "stay," which will protect you at least for a short period of time from attempts by your creditors to collect their debts, evict you from your apartment, or foreclose on your home, subject to the same exceptions as in Chapter 7.

Are there the same meetings?

Just as in Chapter 7, you will be required to attend a meeting with your creditors — the so-called section 341 meeting — at which you will be examined under oath by the Chapter 13 trustee and any creditors who may choose to attend. Also, creditors may ask the court for permission to ask you further questions under oath. This is called a 2004 examination. These examinations are discussed in more detail in part 6.

What are the main differences between the two chapters?

There are two big differences between filing under Chapter 7 and filing a Chapter 13 petition:

1. Unlike Chapter 7, the Chapter 13 stay may also protect spouses, family members, or coworkers who have cosigned or guaranteed consumer loans for you while you repay the creditor whose debt is guaranteed through your Chapter 13 plan. This protection is not absolute. See part 15 for a more complete discussion.

2. You must file a Chapter 13 plan with your petition or within fifteen days after filing (there is no plan in Chapter 7) *and* you must start making payments under your plan within thirty days of filing it.

What happens to the plan I file?

You will be required to attend a hearing at which time the court will consider confirming your plan. If your plan is confirmed, you will be required to make payments to the Chapter 13 trustee for the duration of your plan.

And what happens after the plan is over?

Once payments under your plan have been completed—and it may be that your plan will take as many as sixty months to complete — you will be entitled to a discharge of all dischargeable debts provided for by the plan. You should review part 9 to see if any of your debts are nondischargeable. The most common types of nondischargeable debts involve student loans, alimony and support obligations, and criminal penalties. (The extent of the Chapter 13 discharge will be discussed in more detail below.)

How important is my Chapter 13 plan?

The success of your Chapter 13 plan will depend upon your ability to pay for your basic needs, such as food and shelter, and how much money you will have left over to use to pay your creditors. It will also depend upon the strength of your commitment to repay your creditors.

Schedules I and J to the Official Forms allow you to collect the information you will need to determine if a plan is possible. Copies of those forms are at the end of the book. (Because of the importance of the plan, it gets a separate part of this book — part 8.)

How do I pay for my plan?

Your plan must provide that the Chapter 13 trustee will be able to supervise and control the funds necessary to fund your plan. Although these funds are normally from future income, the Bankruptcy Code does not limit the source of the funds. Consequently, the sale of all or a part of your assets may provide some of the funds necessary to fund your plan.

And how do I get my plan confirmed?

Copies of your plan, or summaries of it, are sent to all of your creditors and the Chapter 13 trustee. Your creditors and the Chapter 13 trustee must also receive a notice of the time, date, and location of the hearing on confirmation of your plan. Any party who objects to your plan must file a copy of that objection with the court and mail your attorney a copy, so you will be able to respond to the objection at the confirmation hearing.

What if no one objects?

Even if none of your creditors objects to your proposed plan, it must still satisfy the six Bankruptcy Code criteria for confirmation. If your plan meets those criteria, and there are no objections, the court must confirm it. The criteria are:

1. Your plan must comply with the provisions of Chapter 13 and all the provisions of the Bankruptcy Code. This means, by way of example, that your plan must not extend payments beyond sixty months; must not provide for partial, instead of full, payment of tax and any other priority claims; and

must not treat undersecured claims as fully secured. This list is by no means exhaustive, but it does represent some of the things the court will be looking into at the confirmation hearing.

2. You must have paid the $120 filing fee, the $30 administrative fee, any other court charges, and any deposits required by your plan. If you have obtained permission to pay the filing fee in installments and the last one or two installments are not yet due, the court, in its discretion, may still confirm your plan.

Other charges that might be payable include charges for copying and certifying documents. However, since those types of fees usually are collected at the time you request the services from the clerk at the Bankruptcy Court, that should not be a problem.

Finally, if your plan provides that certain amounts of money are to be paid to a class of creditors or posted as a deposit, your plan cannot be confirmed unless you are in a position to pay the money or post the deposit.

3. Your plan must have been proposed in good faith and not by any means forbidden by law. This means that a Chapter 13 plan will not be confirmed if, for example, you lie in preparing the schedules and statement of affairs, fail to disclose material facts about your financial affairs, or transfer property in fraud on creditors.

4. The fourth criterion incorporates a standard known as "the best interests of creditors" test. Since

unsecured creditors do not vote to accept or reject your plan, this condition protects their interests. Satisfaction of the test requires a finding by the court that you are distributing property (usually making payments from your future earnings or income) to unsecured creditors through your plan that is not less than the amount of money that they would receive if your Chapter 13 case were converted to a case under Chapter 7, and a Chapter 7 trustee sold all your nonexempt property for the benefit of your creditors.

In applying the "best interests of creditors" test, most courts will think in terms of a hypothetical sale of your nonexempt property on the date you filed your Chapter 13 petition. Courts will compare the present value of the amount of money likely to be received from such a sale with the amount of money you are proposing to distribute to your unsecured creditors through your plan. The hypothetical Chapter 7 sale must account for the administrative and sale expenses of the Chapter 7 trustee, as well as all secured and priority claims.

The present value of the property you intend to distribute is required because a direct comparison between the Chapter 7 sale amount and the total amount you intend to distribute through your plan would not account for the loss of interest resulting from paying your creditors over time.

The simplest way to understand how the present-value analysis works is to think of a Chapter 7 case in which your unsecured creditors would be paid 100 percent of their claims from the sale of your nonexempt assets. The "best interests of creditors" test would not be met if your Chapter 13 plan proposed to pay your unsecured creditors 100 percent of their claims over thirty-six months without interest, since the unsecured creditors in your Chapter 13 case would have lost the opportunity to invest the money they would have received from the hypothetical sale in the Chapter 7 case. In such circumstances, the court would not confirm the Chapter 13 plan.

5. If your Chapter 13 plan does not provide for secured claims, creditors holding secured claims may move for relief from the automatic stay to enforce their rights. If you do provide for secured claims in your plan, your plan can be confirmed if you satisfy one of three tests in the alternative:

   a. the holders of the secured claims accept (or fail to object to) the plan;

   b. the plan provides that the creditors retain their liens or receive the value of their allowed secured claims on the effective date of the plan; or

   c. you surrender the property securing the claim to the holder of the secured claim.

   These three alternatives depend upon the claimant's holding an allowed secured claim. To obtain an allowed secured claim and be afforded the protection of the Bankruptcy Code with respect to the confirmation of Chapter 13 plans, the holder must file a proof of claim. If necessary, there must be a determination of whether the claimant has a fully secured or partially secured claim, a decision that will depend upon the value of the collateral securing the claim.

The first alternative is simple. If a secured creditor receives the appropriate notice of the plan and the confirmation hearing and either accepts the plan or fails to object to it, the first test is satisfied.

The third alternative test is also fairly simple. You can simply give the property that secures the claim back to the secured creditor before or at the time of confirmation. The claimant would be free to sell the collateral in a commercially reasonable manner. If the net proceeds of the sale do not pay the amount due to the creditor in full, the creditor can assert an *unsecured* claim for the unpaid balance.

The second alternative treatment of secured claims is extremely complex and is known as a "cramdown." First, the judge must determine the present value of the property to be distributed under the plan. As an example, if the present value of the property you are retaining is $100, and you owe $150 on it, you might propose to pay the $100 in ten monthly payments of $10 each from your earnings or other future income. The court must then convert the total sum of deferred payments into a capitalized sum as of the effective date of the plan.

The "capitalized sum" will be somewhat smaller than the total of all the payments to be made — $100 payable at the rate of $10 per month is worth less to the creditor than $100 paid in a lump sum today.

Having done that, the court determines an appropriate interest rate that you must pay in addition to the $10 payments to bring the present value of the payments up to the value of the theoretical lump sum. The object is to put the secured creditor in the same position it would be in if you surrendered the collateral securing the claim. If you had simply returned the property, the creditor could have sold it right away for $100. The payment of interest compensates the secured creditor for the delay in receiving the money it would have obtained if the property had been surrendered and immediately sold.

6. The final test is feasibility. The court must find that you will be able to make all the payments called for under your plan and that you will be able to comply with the terms of your plan.

Now that I know the law, what are the practicalities of putting together a plan?

One of the duties of the Chapter 13 trustee is to determine whether your financial circumstances will permit confirmation of the plan you initially propose. If you start making plan payments within thirty days after the filing of your plan, as required by the Bankruptcy Code, the Chapter 13 trustee will be in a position to know if you have the ability to make your plan payments. If you follow his or her advice, the finding of feasibility should not be a problem.

What if someone objects to my plan for one of the reasons you just set out?

If an unsecured creditor or the Chapter 13 trustee objects to your plan for failure to comply with one of the points outlined above, not only will you have to address the objection, but the court will have to make additional findings. In other words, if there are any objections to your plan, the court cannot confirm your plan unless it finds either

1. that the value of property being distributed under the plan will pay the claim of the objecting party in full; or
2. that you propose to pay into your plan all of your disposable income for three years beginning on the date the first payment under the plan is due.

Wait a moment, what is "disposable income"?

The Bankruptcy Code defines disposable income as "income received by the debtor and which is not reasonably necessary to be expended . . . for the maintenance or support of the debtor or a dependent of the debtor." If you are engaged in business, the Code expands the definition to include expenditures required for "the continuation, preservation, and operation of such business."

Can just anyone raise that issue?

There are several points that should be noted with respect to the disposable-income test. First, only unsecured creditors and the Chapter 13 trustee can object to your plan on the grounds that you have not allocated all of your disposable income to the payment of claims. Second, only parties who have in fact filed claims can object.

The application of the disposable-income test is a nearly impossible task for the judge. Application of the test with precision would require lengthy trials and expert witnesses, and, frankly, in the usual case, that is just not going to happen. As a result, the court may simply multiply your income and expenses by the number of months that payments are going to be made to determine whether the test has been satisfied. Before doing this, the court may scrutinize your expenses to see if in fact they are reasonable.

Although the court should not be concerned with imposing its own values on you, or making dramatic changes to your lifestyle by ruling that certain expenditures are unnecessary, it is clear that the court will focus on your consumption of luxury goods and services. As a Chapter 13 debtor, it is unlikely that the court will sanction payments for an expensive pleasure boat or the very latest model Cadillac when a Chevy would do just fine. The feeling is that it is not fair that your unsecured creditors make sacrifices in terms of when and how much they will be paid, when you are unwilling to make personal sacrifices yourself. The court will not confirm a plan that encompasses such an unjust result under either the disposable-income test or the good-faith test discussed above.

Does the court control my income?

In connection with the confirmation of your plan or after confirmation, the court may issue payment orders against your employer, your pension fund, or government agencies paying you benefits (except the Social Security Administration). The court might enter such an order for one of two reasons: administrative convenience and elimination of the risk that your Chapter 13 plan will be impaired through diversion of funds.

What is the effect of confirmation of my plan?

The confirmation of your plan has two significant effects. First, it binds you and your creditors whether or not the claims of your creditors have been provided for in your plan and whether or not the creditors have objected to, accepted, or rejected your plan. Second, it vests all of the property of your bankruptcy estate in you, free and clear of the claims or interests of any creditors provided for in the plan (except for secured creditors to the extent that the plan covers them).

What is the importance of the order confirming my plan?

The binding effect of the order confirming your plan highlights the importance of giving notice to all creditors. Once your plan has been confirmed, creditors who have failed to object to it will be out of luck. After confirmation, creditors provided for in the plan will be limited to the rights given to them under the plan. They will not be able collect their debts by foreclosure or the commencement of a lawsuit in the state courts. Moreover, the automatic stay remains in effect until payments under your plan have been completed, although a creditor may be able to obtain relief from the stay if you fail to make your plan payments. Another exception to the automatic stay may pertain to collection of postpetition alimony and child-support payments.

Once I've had my plan confirmed and started making payments, are my obligations graven in stone?

After your Chapter 13 plan has been confirmed, but before you have completed all payments, you may be able to obtain the permission of the court to modify your plan. The Chapter 13 trustee, or the holder of an allowed unsecured claim, also may request modification. Notice to the Chapter 13 trustee and to all your creditors (or at least those creditors affected by the modification) and a hearing are required. If the court allows you to modify your plan, which the court will only do if the modified plan satisfies all the requirements for confirmation outlined above, the plan as modified becomes the plan.

What would motivate me to change my plan?

Changes in your financial circumstances that were not anticipated at the time of the original confirmation hearing usually prompt the filing of a modified plan or a request to modify your plan. Your plan may be modified

1. to increase or decrease the amount of payments on claims of a particular class,
2. to extend or reduce the time for such payments, or
3. to alter the amount of the distribution to a creditor whose claim is provided for under the plan to the extent necessary to take into account payment of the claim other than under the plan.

Is there a danger I might lose the benefit of my plan?

The Bankruptcy Code provides that, on the request of a party in interest, the order confirming a Chapter 13 plan can be revoked if the order was procured by fraud. The request must be made within 180 days of the date the confirmation order was entered. Further, if the order is revoked, the Bankruptcy Code directs the court to either convert the case to Chapter 7 or dismiss it, unless the debtor proposes and the court confirms a modified plan.

What if I no longer need the protection of Chapter 13?

A Chapter 13 case can be converted to another chapter or dismissed either by your own action or by motion of the Chapter 13 trustee or a creditor.

If you file a Chapter 13 instead of a Chapter 7 and you decide that you do not want or need the protection of Chapter 13 any longer, you can dismiss your Chapter 13 case or convert your Chapter 13 case to a case under Chapter 7 *at any time.* This is not the case in a Chapter 7 proceeding, in which the Trustee and all your creditors must be given notice and an opportunity to object to dismissal.

What if someone else asks the court to convert or dismiss my Chapter 13 case?

The Chapter 13 trustee or a creditor may request the court to convert or dismiss your Chapter 13 case. If this happens, the court will schedule a hearing. All your creditors must receive notice of this hearing and be given an opportunity to object. The Bankruptcy Code lists several grounds for conversion or dismissal of a Chapter 13 case. However, the court may convert or dismiss a case, whichever is in the best interests of your creditors, and for other reasons as well. The reasons set forth in the Bankruptcy Code include:

1. unreasonable delay that is prejudicial to creditors;
2. nonpayment of fees and charges;
3. failure to timely file a plan;
4. failure to commence making payments within thirty days of the filing of your plan;
5. denial of confirmation and denial of a request made for additional time in which to file a plan;
6. a material default with respect to the terms of a confirmed plan;
7. revocation of the order confirming a Chapter 13 plan and denial of confirmation of a modified plan;
8. termination of a confirmed plan by reason of an occurrence specified in the plan other than completion of payments;
9. failure to file a list of creditors, schedules, and a statement of financial affairs.

Your Chapter 13 case can be converted to Chapter 11 or Chapter 12 upon the request of a party in interest and after notice to all creditors and a hearing. However, the request to convert to those chapters must be made prior to confirmation of your Chapter 13 plan, and you must be eligible to be a debtor under those two chapters. If you are a farmer, you can convert your case to Chapter 7, 11, or 12, but you cannot be forced into another chapter.

What happens if my plan is converted or dismissed?

If your case is converted to Chapter 7 of the Bankruptcy Code, the conversion will vacate any order entered confirming your Chapter 13 plan. Any debts you incurred after filing your Chapter 13 plan, but before conversion, will be treated as prepetition claims in your Chapter 7 case and may be discharged. Any property you acquired after filing your Chapter 13 case may be treated differently, depending upon where you file your bankruptcy petition. The better view is that the property does not become part of your Chapter 7 estate, but not all bankruptcy judges agree with that position.

What happens if my case is dismissed?

If your case is dismissed, you will not receive a discharge of any of your debts, and the order of dismissal will undo certain actions taken during your bankruptcy, except sales of your property authorized by the bankruptcy court to people or businesses that bought in good faith. In most instances the dismissal does not stop you from filing again, short of a violation of the good-faith requirements. However, if your Chapter 13 case is dismissed because you failed to abide by a court order, or you voluntarily dismissed your case after a motion for relief from stay has been filed by a creditor, you are prohibited from filing another bankruptcy case for 180 days after the dismissal.

What types of discharge can I get in Chapter 13?

There are two types of discharge that can be obtained in a Chapter 13 case:

1. the full-compliance discharge; and
2. the hardship discharge.

What is a full-compliance discharge?

After you have completed all payments under your plan, the Chapter 13 trustee should begin the process of obtaining a discharge order for you. The discharge that you obtain will be broader than the discharge you can obtain by filing a petition in Chapter 7. The broad discharge applicable in Chapter 13 reflects a congressional intent to give you and all Chapter 13 debtors every incentive to complete plan payments. Thus, debts for willful and malicious torts and debts for which a discharge could be denied in Chapter 7 may be discharged in Chapter 13.

A full-compliance discharge discharges all claims provided for under the plan and all claims disallowed by the court. Moreover, the claims of creditors, including priority creditors, who have failed to file claims will be discharged as long as the plan contains some provision describing the treatment of those claims, and no exception to discharge applies.

Are there any exceptions?

The exceptions to the full-compliance discharge include certain long-term debts provided for in your plan. The Bankruptcy Code allows you to make special provision for curing defaults and maintaining payments on secured or unsecured debts in which the last contract payment would be due after the completion of your Chapter 13 plan. Those debts are not discharged.

Debts for alimony, maintenance, or support, as well as certain debts for student loans and debts for death or personal injury caused by your operation of a motor vehicle while intoxicated, are also excepted from discharge. These matters are discussed more fully in part 9.

Another type of debt excepted from discharge is one for restitution included in a sentence on your conviction of a crime. If the restitution order does not result from a conviction but rather from some other proceeding or agreement, the restitution debt can be discharged.

Finally, debts you incur after the filing of your Chapter 13 petition and not provided for in your Chapter 13 plan are not discharged. However, Chapter 13 permits certain postpetition claims to be treated as prepetition claims. Accordingly, any governmental unit may file a claim for taxes that became payable to it while your case is pending. The same is true for consumer debts for property or services necessary for you to perform your plan. These claims will be treated as prepetition claims for purposes of proof, allowance, and priority.

If you have such postpetition debts and if you have provided for them in your plan, the Chapter 13 discharge will let you off the hook on those claims in most cases. However, if a claim is filed for a consumer debt, the holder of which knew or should have known that the prior approval of the Chapter 13 trustee was practicable, then that claim is disallowed. The Chapter 13 provision providing for the disallowance of the consumer-debt claim is designed to protect you from incurring unnecessary debt that you lack the means to repay, or credit obtained on unfavorable terms.

What is a hardship discharge?

Even if you fail to complete all payments under your confirmed Chapter 13 plan, you may still obtain what is called a hardship discharge. You will have to file a motion to obtain this type of discharge, and there will have to be a hearing with notice given to all your creditors. There are three conditions for obtaining a hardship discharge:

1. your failure or inability to complete all plan payments must be due to circumstances for which you should not be held accountable;
2. the court must find that the value, on the effective date of the plan, of property actually distributed to unsecured creditors is not less than the amount that would have been paid to them if your estate had been liquidated on the effective date of the plan (this is a variation of the "best interests of creditors" test discussed above); and
3. modification of your Chapter 13 plan is impractical.

The hardship discharge is far less sweeping than the full-compliance discharge. You can be relieved from liability for unsecured debts that have been disallowed or that were provided for in your plan, but not secured debts or postpetition consumer debts. Just as in the case of a full-compliance discharge, you will not receive a discharge for certain long-term debts provided for in your plan. Most important, you will not be discharged from any debts discussed in part 9. The most important are: most taxes; "improperly" incurred debts; debts not scheduled; fraud as a fiduciary; alimony and child support; willful and malicious acts; fines, penalties, and forfeitures; student loans; and damages caused while operating a motor vehicle while intoxicated.

When I've received a discharge I'm home free, right?

Not necessarily. A party in interest may ask the court to revoke your discharge within one year of your receiving it. The court may revoke your discharge only after a hearing and only if you obtained the discharge through fraud and the party requesting the revocation did not learn of the fraud until after the discharge.

Does getting a Chapter 13 discharge mean it's all over?

A Chapter 13 discharge does not affect your ability to seek further relief under either Chapter 13 or Chapter 11 of the Bankruptcy Code. However, you may not be able to obtain a discharge in a Chapter 7 case if your Chapter 13 discharge is within six years of the filing of a Chapter 7, unless payments under your plan totalled at least 70 percent of the allowed unsecured claims, and the Chapter 13 plan was proposed in good faith and constituted your "best effort."

PART

8

Preparing Your Chapter 13 Plan

There is no official form for a Chapter 13 plan. However, the information in your plan should be consistent with the information you provided in your schedules and Statement of Affairs. At a minimum, the plan should contain the following:

1. The complete name and address of your employer (if any) to whom a payroll deduction order may be sent;
2. The amount of payments into the plan, their source, frequency, and duration;
3. A statement of all secured claims that are to be paid through the plan; the amount of the secured claims; the amount to be paid each holder of a secured claim, and the interest rate;
4. The amount of all priority claims, and the schedule for paying them in full;

5. The proposed classification of unsecured claims, and the percentage or amount that will be paid to the holders of unsecured claims;
6. A statement as to any payments that will be made outside the plan or directly to any creditors;
7. The disposition of any leases;
8. A statement as to what if any property you intend to surrender or transfer;
9. The amount of money you intend to pay any attorneys you have hired; and
10. A provision for the payment of postpetition claims.

The most important thing to keep in mind when you sit down to draft your Chapter 13 plan is to have the proposed plan payments fit within your budget. It's a mistake to try to make your budget fit your plan in an attempt to make your creditors happy. You will not succeed. To work, your plan must be based on a practical review of your income and your expenses. The amount left over after the payment of your expenses must sustain your plan. If that sum is inadequate, then you should consider filing a Chapter 7 petition.

Most Chapter 13 debtors must consider the following types of debt: priority claims, including taxes, secured claims, and unsecured claims. In the next few paragraphs each of these types of claims are discussed.

PRIORITY CLAIMS

Priority claims must be paid in full to obtain confirmation of your Chapter 13 plan, unless the holder of the claim

agrees to a different treatment. The Bankruptcy Code identifies seven different types of priority claims. The most
common ones are unsecured tax claims, attorneys' fees,
trustees' fees, and filing fees. Except for the filing fees and
expenses associated with the administration of your bankruptcy case, priority claims need not be paid in any particular order or at any particular time while your Chapter 13
case is pending, although it is a very good idea to get your
priority claims paid before you start paying your unsecured
claims.

A typical type of tax claim entitled to priority is one for
income taxes for a tax year for which a return was due
within three years of the date you file your petition. Other
types of taxes entitled to priority are property taxes assessed
before you filed for bankruptcy protection and payable
within the year before you filed. Property taxes secured by
a lien are different and not entitled to the same treatment as
priority tax claims. Although priority tax claims are not entitled to postpetition interest, interest that accrued prior to
the filing is part of the claim and must be paid. Likewise,
prepetition tax penalties may be entitled to the same priority as the underlying tax claim. However, this depends on
whether the penalty is compensatory or punitive. If it is the
latter, the penalty is just an unsecured claim that does not
have to be paid in full.

Debtors engaged in business may have to be concerned
with claims for withholding employees' taxes and sales
taxes. These types of liabilities may arise from involvement
as a responsible officer in a corporation.

Tax issues and the consequences of their inappropriate
resolution are frequently intimidating and complex. If your

tax situation is at all confusing, you should seek the assistance of counsel, as the filing of a bankruptcy petition will not automatically resolve your tax problems, and, indeed, in some circumstances it may compound them.

The Bankruptcy Code contemplates that priority claims will be paid in deferred cash payments. This gives you some leeway. You can propose to make the payments monthly or quarterly over the life of the plan. However, it is to your advantage to provide for the payment of priority claims first through your plan.

SECURED CLAIMS

In general, if you desire to keep property that serves as collateral (any type of property that serves as security for the repayment of a debt) for a prepetition debt, you must pay the creditor its value through the plan. Your plan must provide that your secured creditors retain their liens and that the payments you propose equal the present value of the collateral securing the claims and meet the rate of depreciation during the period of delayed payments. Of course, you have the option of surrendering the collateral and giving the creditor an unsecured claim for any deficiency with respect to the value of the collateral. It may even be appropriate for you to sell the collateral. However, this avenue is not without complications that may require the assistance of counsel.

It is possible for you to modify the terms and interest rate applicable to secured claims, except a secured claim secured only by real estate that is your principal residence. Generally, in situations where the principal residence exception does not apply, the amount of the claim is reduced to the value of the collateral, the interest rate is changed, and the number of payments is changed to fit within your budget and the plan. To accomplish this, the value of the collateral must be determined. Without the consent of the secured party, this might involve costly and time-consuming litigation. Moreover, your payments must account for the depreciation in the value of the collateral.

HOME MORTGAGES

Some courts used to allow debtors to bifurcate or split a claim secured by a first mortgage on their residences into secured and unsecured portions. For example, if the amount of the first mortgage was $150,000 and the value of the house was $125,000, the holder of the first mortgage would have two claims: a secured claim in the amount of $125,000 and an unsecured claim for $25,000. The consequence of this was that although the debtor had to continue to make the same monthly payments, the term of the loan was shortened because effectively the debtor owed less money. This is no longer permissible in the case of mortgages secured only by a debtor's principal residence.

The Supreme Court of the United States has ruled that the Bankruptcy Code prohibits you from modifying the mortgage on your principal residence. Consequently, you generally have the option of surrendering your home to the creditor that holds the mortgage or making up all your late payments — "curing the arrearages" in bankruptcy jargon, and then making the regular monthly payments due under the note. The Supreme Court held that the Bankruptcy

Code prohibits Chapter 13 debtors from reducing an undersecured mortgage (one in which the value of the property is less than the amount of the secured debt) to the fair market value of the residence. A mortgage lender's rights, which may include the right to repayment, the right to retain the lien, the right to accelerate the loan, and the right to foreclose in its documents, are enforceable regardless of whether the creditor is undersecured or not. However, the Supreme Court has yet to resolve the issue of whether interest must be paid on arrearages.

Thus, to keep your home in a Chapter 13 if there have been defaults, you must reinstate the original loan by curing the arrearages and maintain the payments called for in the original loan during the life of the plan and after its completion. In other words, you cannot change the interest rate, and you must abide by all nonmonetary provisions contained in your loan agreements as well. Your attorney will know whether you must also pay interest on arrearages.

There are some exceptions to the rule as stated above, however. For example, if the secured creditor has collateral other than your principal residence securing the loan, then you may be able to modify the terms of the mortgage. Likewise, if your residence is also used for business purposes, you might be able to modify the terms of the loan. Nevertheless, given the size of most mortgages and the requirements outlined above, namely that you must pay the present value during the life of the plan, and that you must compensate the lender for depreciation in the value of the property, it may not be worth your effort to litigate the issue. Thus, the only practical approach in most instances is to cure the defaults and reinstate the terms of the original loan. Trying to get an end run around the protection afforded banks or institutional lenders holding first mortgages on your personal residence is only warranted where the size of the loan is relatively small, the interest rate is unfavorable, and one of the exceptions outlined above is applicable.

UNSECURED CLAIMS

Examples of unsecured claims are credit card debts, debts arising from breach or rejection of certain leases or contracts, and deficiency claims — the difference between the value of property securing a debt and the face amount of the debt.

The Bankruptcy Code provides that you can put the claims of unsecured creditors in different classes. However, you can only obtain confirmation of your Chapter 13 plan as long as you don't unfairly discriminate against any particular class of unsecured claims. This means that you can't decide to pay one credit card company its claim in full and not pay another credit card company at all or to some lesser extent. Moreover, each holder of an unsecured claim must receive no less than what it would receive if you had decided to file a Chapter 7 case. For example, if you owned a house worth $200,000, subject to a mortgage of $100,000, and you had $20,000 of unsecured debt, you could not propose a plan that would satisfy the secured debt and pay your unsecured creditors 10 cents on the dollar. The reason is that if your house were to be sold by a Chapter 7 trustee and the mortgage were to be paid, there would still be well over $20,000 available to satisfy your unsecured creditors even after the payment of a federal exemption amount, such costs of the sale as the broker's commission, and the trustee's fees. Under these facts, you would have to pay your unsecured claims in full.

With respect to how you classify claims, the Bankruptcy Code merely provides that the claims in each class must be substantially similar to one another. Courts have not been uniform in their interpretation of that language. You will be safe if you treat all unsecured claims, other than priority claims, in the same way.

MODIFICATION OF YOUR PLAN PRIOR TO CONFIRMATION

You may modify your plan any time prior to confirmation without the court's permission, and the plan as modified becomes your plan. So, if your financial circumstances change for better or for worse, or if, after negotiating with creditors, you will be able to avoid objections to your plan, you may modify your plan. The plan as modified must comply with the provisions of Chapter 13. If you modify your plan, however, you must notify any creditor who will be worse off because of the modification and give that creditor at least twenty days' notice to accept or reject your modified plan. A secured creditor's acceptance or rejection of your initial plan is binding unless the modified plan changes its rights. The court may be called upon to make that finding prior to or at the time of confirmation.

IMPORTANT PLAN PROVISIONS

To summarize, the following is a list of provisions that you *must* include in your Chapter 13 plan:

1. you must provide for the submission to the Chapter 13 trustee of all or such portion of your future earnings or income as is necessary for the execution of your plan;
2. you must provide for full payment of claims entitled to priority, unless the holder consents to a different treatment;
3. you must provide for the similar treatment of all claims in the same class; and
4. you must provide for payments over a period no longer than thirty-six months unless the court for cause allows you to extend your plan to a maximum of sixty months.

Subject to those four absolute requirements, you may do any of the following in your Chapter 13 plan:

1. designate a class or classes of unsecured claims (claims involving co-debtors may be classified separately);
2. modify the rights of holders of secured claims, other than a claim secured *only* by a security interest in your principal residence;
3. modify the rights of holders of unsecured claims;
4. leave the rights of holders of any class of claims unaffected;
5. provide for the cure or waiving of any default, usually with respect to secured claims (the cure or waiver of a default is not a modification);

6. provide for concurrent payments of secured, unsecured, and priority claims;

7. notwithstanding the right to modify secured claims, provide for the curing of any default within a reasonable time, and the maintenance of payments on any secured or unsecured claim on which the last payment will come due after the date on which your final plan payment will come due (with such a provision in your plan, you can cure arrearages through your plan and make the regular payment to the creditor directly, thereby avoiding Chapter 13 trustee commissions and getting the creditor paid somewhat faster);

8. provide for the payment of all or any part of an allowed postpetition claim;

9. subject to the provisions of the Bankruptcy Code, provide for the assumption or rejection of certain types of contracts and leases;

10. provide for payment of all or part of a claim from the sale of property;

11. provide for the vesting of property of the estate in you or another entity at confirmation or at some later time; and

12. provide that confirmation of your plan shall constitute a finding by the court that the plan is your best effort toward the repayment of your debts (such a provision would come in handy if you were in a position to have to seek a hardship discharge, a circumstance that is discussed in detail in part 7).

PART

9

Getting a Discharge; Nondischargeable Debts

The words are almost the same, and there is a great deal of confusion between the two concepts: *discharge* and *dischargeability*. In bankruptcy the difference is very important.

What do you mean by "starting over" in bankruptcy?

The primary goal of the bankruptcy laws is the fresh start: allowing debtors to wipe out old obligations and start over. The event that makes the fresh start possible is the *discharge* — an order of the Bankruptcy Court freeing a person from responsibility for prior debts.

What is the meaning of a discharge?

The effect of a discharge is to remove liability for prefiling debts in general. It also puts in place a permanent in-

73

junction against prefiling creditors, prohibiting them from seeking to collect obligations that were discharged.

Does it differ from dischargeability?

Dischargeability, on the other hand, refers to a single, particular obligation, and the question of whether that particular debt can be wiped out. You can obtain a discharge from all but one, or all but a few, debts.

In a Chapter 7 case, if no complaints objecting to discharge are filed, the discharge order issues "forthwith" upon expiration of the time for filing objections to discharge, sixty days after the section 341 meeting described in part 6. In proceedings under Chapters 12 and 13, a discharge order follows successful completion of the plan.

Can anyone object to my discharge?

Any creditor, the trustee, or the United States Trustee, may file a formal complaint (and pay a $120 filing fee) alleging facts that constitute grounds for denial of discharge. This is known as "the commencement of an adversary proceeding." The judge, on request of a party, may also direct the trustee to examine the conduct of the debtor to see if grounds exist for denying a discharge.

What reasons are there for denying me a discharge?

The technical details of filing a complaint to discharge are found in part 15 (Information for Creditors). The acts that may cause denial of a *discharge* — remember, this means that *nothing* will be accomplished by the bankruptcy proceeding — are:

1. *Fraudulent transfer, concealment, or destruction of property.* If a debtor, within the year before, or at any

time after, the filing of the petition, with intent to hinder, delay, or defraud creditors (intent may be inferred from the debtor's actions), has transferred, destroyed, mutilated, or concealed property, or permitted that to be done, the discharge may be denied.

In part 12, both "fraudulent transfers" and the trustee's ability to recover transferred property from other persons are discussed. In part 16, property transfers that may constitute bankruptcy crimes are discussed. What we are dealing with here is the other side of the transaction — the effect that making the transfer has on the debtor's right to a discharge. The definitions in the present section are in many respects broader than those covered by part 12.

2. *Failure to keep records or destruction of records.* Debtors are supposed to have records from which their financial condition and business transactions can be ascertained. If the debtor does not keep such records, or falsifies, conceals, or destroys them, a discharge may be denied. It may be possible to justify destruction of records, but that is a difficult burden in most cases.

3. *False oath or claim.* Debtors take oaths when they sign their bankruptcy petitions and related documents, when they testify at the section 341 meeting, and when they otherwise testify in connection with their case. A knowing and willful falsehood may result in denial of discharge.

4. *Bribery.* Knowingly and fraudulently offering, giving, or receiving a bribe in connection with the bankruptcy case may result in denial of discharge.

5. *Failure to cooperate with the trustee.* A debtor who knowingly and fraudulently withholds information from the trustee may be denied a discharge.

6. *Failure to explain loss of assets.* If the debtor at one time had assets that have disappeared, and can offer no satisfactory explanation for their absence, discharge may be denied.

7. *Failure to obey valid orders.* A debtor must obey any lawful order of the Bankruptcy Court. This may include attending examinations, producing documents, or otherwise providing relevant information. Subject to the debtor's right to claim the privilege against self- incrimination under the Fifth Amendment, disobedience of a court order is grounds for denial of discharge. The claim of rights under the Fifth Amendment, as a practical matter, protects against criminal prosecutions, but may well have an adverse effect on discharge.

8. *Forbidden acts in another bankruptcy case.* If the debtor has committed any of the acts listed above within the year prior to the filing of the bankruptcy petition, or at any time after filing, or in connection with the bankruptcy case of someone else who is an "insider" of the debtor in the present case, discharge may be denied. "Insider" is explained in detail in part 12. In brief, the term includes relatives of the debtor, any partnerships in which the debtor is a general partner, the other general part-

ners in partnership with the present debtor, relatives of those general partners, and any corporation of which the present debtor is a director, officer, or controlling person.

Are there any debts that will not die, that simply survive bankruptcy?

Certain debts cannot be discharged in bankruptcy. In many instances, the issue doesn't even have to be raised by the creditor, the debt simply survives. In others, a creditor must object to the dischargeability of its debt within sixty days of the first date set for the section 341 meeting. The types of debts for which dischargeability complaints must be filed within sixty days include debts for fraud, embezzlement, larceny, and willful, and malicious injuries (see paragraphs 2, 4, and 6 below).

Remember that dischargeability speaks only about a particular obligation. The fact that a debt is nondischargeable does not affect the discharge of other obligations.

The nondischargeable debts most often applicable in a personal bankruptcy are:

1. *Most taxes.* If you owe federal income taxes that were due for at least three years before you filed your bankruptcy petition and they are for a period when you properly filed your tax return, the taxes may be dischargeable. With that singular exception, you should consider all taxes, state and federal, to be nondischargeable. In other words, you'll have to pay them anyway. So, if a debtor's principal obliga-

tions are for taxes, there is little point in seeking relief in bankruptcy.

Some taxes, such as real estate taxes due more than a year before the bankruptcy filing, can be discharged as a technical matter, but that has no practical significance. The property taxes carry with them liens that automatically attach to the property against which they are assessed. The assessment lives on, and you will be unable to sell the property, or get a new mortgage, without paying the taxes, even if they have been discharged.

2. *"Improperly" incurred debts.* The technical legal term is "fraudulently incurred debts," but it covers things far beyond what non-lawyers consider to be fraudulent. We'll use the proper term for the rest of this discussion, but the hint of the topic headline — impropriety — will still give you a better idea.

If a creditor objects, and sustains the burden of proof in the adversary proceeding that must be commenced, debts incurred for activities that the law considers to be fraudulent will not be discharged.

The primary group consists of acts that demonstrate an intent to hurt the creditor. It works this way: if you obtain services, goods, or money on credit, the law says that you are representing to the seller that you can pay the bill when it is due. If the facts are clear that you knew you'd never be able to pay when due, you probably have incurred a non-dischargeable debt. Some examples are:

- Writing a check in payment of a debt when you know there isn't enough money in the bank.
- Stopping payment on a check so that it won't bounce.
- Lying about how much you owe, or your income, or other financial information. You can get caught on this one by a statement in writing as well as by a false financial statement.
- Credit card abuse, such as using your charge card when you know you can't make the monthly payments, after you have been told to return the card, or for luxuries just before you file for bankruptcy.

There is a specific provision in the Bankruptcy Code dealing with "loading up" before filing. If you run up debts for luxury goods or services of more than $500 with a single creditor within forty days before filing, it is presumed that you intended to defraud the creditor. For this purpose, buying from a number of stores but charging it on a single charge card is treated as buying from a single creditor. Cash advances of more than $1,000 taken on a credit card less than twenty days before filing are generally nondischargeable under the same statutory provision.

There was a time when credit card companies and major stores just "wrote it off" if you filed bankruptcy. Because of the increasing rate of defaults and bankruptcy filings today, these creditors are becoming much more active in opposing discharge when they can make a reasonable case.

3. *Debts not scheduled.* Creditors must be given notice of the filing of a bankruptcy case so that they can file a proof of claim, or object to the discharge, or to the dischargeability of their particular debt. If a creditor does not have notice, the debt generally will not be discharged.

That is the reason why persons contemplating bankruptcy must be so very careful to list as creditors not only the obvious ones, but also all persons and firms who claim they are creditors, even if their claims are disputed or just plain silly.

It is sometimes possible to amend the schedules to correct omissions, but there can be a lot of rocks on that road.

If a creditor received notice of the filing from the court or the debtor, or received actual notice of it in any other way, the debt may be discharged if the creditor doesn't file a claim or take some other kind of action.

4. *Fraud as a fiduciary.* If you are executor of an estate who steals money from the estate or a real estate broker who pockets down payments instead of putting them into escrow or a lawyer who diverts clients' funds into a personal bank account, the obligation to repay will not be dischargeable.

Although most courts take a very narrow view of what it takes to be a fiduciary, a significant minority of judges apply this exception broadly where the debtor knew that he or she was acting improperly with someone else's money or property that had been entrusted to him or her.

Debts incurred as a result of embezzlement or larceny are not dischargeable either under this category.

5. *Alimony and child support.* This is frequently one of the most complicated areas in the law, because the lawyers who handle divorce proceedings may not have considered the possibility of bankruptcy when they drafted divorce pleadings or property settlement agreements. It is often not clear whether a transfer of property that was supposed to be made by the person who is now in bankruptcy was intended to be alimony or child support (in which case the obligation will continue) or to be a property settlement (which is treated as just another unsecured debt and can be discharged).

6. *Willful and malicious acts.* The statute says that, if a creditor objects, you cannot discharge debts arising from "willful and malicious injury" to another's person or property. It's a very broad phrase and it is intended to be that way.

You can think of the easy examples, such as a judgment for assaulting someone or deliberately damaging that person's car. The harder cases are where, while you didn't act in a truly intentional way, you were so reckless that the law considers you to have intended whatever follows from your conduct. For instance, if you are engaged in a high-speed road race and someone is injured, it's possible that you will be held to have been so reckless that the injury you caused will be ruled to be "willful and malicious."

A lot of things that are crimes can also result in civil liability for damages. The resulting judgment will probably not be dischargeable.

7. *Fines, penalties, and forfeitures.* Fines in criminal proceedings and the like payable to governmental units are not discharged.

8. *Student loans.* Normally, student loans cannot be discharged in bankruptcy. If student loans form a significant part of the debt load, bankruptcy may not be of much assistance. And, if the bankruptcy filing was primarily to get rid of student loan debts, it is probable that the loans will not be discharged, and some courts will even dismiss the case as a bad faith filing.

   There are two exceptions to the no-discharge rule:

   a. If payments on the loan first became due more than seven years before the filing of the bankruptcy petition, the loan can be discharged.

   b. Even if the loan became due during the seven years before filing, it can be discharged if the borrower can demonstrate "undue hardship." This is a very strict test in most courts. Mere inconvenience, the inability to save money, or a temporary physical problem, will not do it.

   An exception to the "undue hardship" rule deals with HEAL loans (Health Education Assistance Loans). Those loans cannot be discharged unless payment would impose "an unconscionable burden" on the debtor. That is a close to impossible burden to satisfy.

9. *Operating while intoxicated.* If you cause personal injury or death while operating a motor vehicle while intoxicated from using alcohol, drugs, or other substances, the liability cannot be discharged in bankruptcy.

10. *Debts previously nondischargeable.* If the debtor was also the debtor in a prior bankruptcy case, and that case was dismissed because of fraud, or the debtor waived discharge in the earlier case, debts that were not discharged in the earlier case are not dischargeable in the new one.

PART

10

Dealing with Leases and Other Executory Contracts

People sometimes sign leases for residential or personal property that result in extreme hardship. For example, the $2,000 monthly rent for an apartment was not a problem when both husband and wife were working, but it is much more than they can afford when one of them is laid off. The same might be true of a leased car or other personal property.

The Bankruptcy Code provides help by allowing the rejection of "executory contracts," which include most leases, but at a price that will be discussed later. The term "executory contract" includes other agreements that are continuing with obligations due on both sides, such as the agreement between a franchisor and its franchisees. This part will just discuss leases; the other kinds of executory contracts are much less common and, when they do exist, are often extremely complex to deal with.

I probably will want to reject that lease; how much time do I have to decide if I do or not?

The debtor in Chapter 13 proceedings has a right to assume or reject an unexpired lease of personal property or residential real estate at any time before the confirmation of a plan. The court may shorten that time if requested to do so by the other party to the lease.

In Chapter 7, the trustee must act within sixty days after the entry of the order for relief, either by assuming or rejecting the lease of residential real estate, or ask the court within the sixty days for additional time in which to do so. The extension is up to the bankruptcy judge. If there is no action within the sixty days or within the extended time period, the lease is automatically deemed rejected.

If I can get out of having to pay so much money, why would I or my trustee ever want to assume a lease?

In Chapter 7, as in Chapter 13, a lease constitutes property of the estate. Therefore, if the lease has value — if, for example, it is a long-term lease for very desirable property at below-market rental rates — the trustee may wish to assume the lease in order to sell it to a third party. If the lease is burdensome, the trustee may want to reject it. If the lease has no value to the Chapter 7 estate, the trustee may abandon the lease as a practical matter by taking no action at all, so that it is deemed rejected.

With respect to apartment leases and leases of personal property, again as a practical matter, the debtor, especially if there are no defaults under the lease, can work out arrangements with the lessor or landlord, although, technically, the lease may have been deemed rejected.

Can my trustee do just anything about the lease?

The trustee must obtain court approval to assume or reject the lease, unless the lease is rejected because nothing was done within the appropriate time period. The decision on whether to assume or reject is based upon the best interest of the estate.

What happens if the lease is assumed?

If the debtor is not in default under the lease (clauses in the lease making filing bankruptcy a default don't count as real defaults), the court will generally allow the Chapter 7 trustee or the Chapter 13 debtor to assume the lease. If there has been a default, assumption will not be granted unless the problem is corrected, including payment of overdue rent, and the trustee or Chapter 13 debtor provides adequate assurance of future performance under the lease. This is called curing the default.

How would I go about curing a default?

Dealing with an apartment lease, for example, cure might consist of paying any rent that had not been paid on time; paying any damages, such as late charges or interest, that the lease requires to be paid; and convincing the bankruptcy judge that there is adequate assurance of proper performance of the terms of the lease in the future. This could be proof that the Chapter 13 debtor's current income is high enough to meet the lease payments.

But seriously, what is the meaning of rejection of the lease?

It is much more common for bankruptcy to be used to reject a lease than to assume it. If a lease is rejected, the other party is given a general unsecured claim against the estate for the amount of damages suffered. There is a limit to the damages, however, in the case of a lease of real property. They cannot exceed unpaid rent plus the lease rent for one to three years, depending upon the remaining term. The lessor also gets the property back.

PART

11

Exemptions

When you file a petition under Chapter 7 or Chapter 13 of the Bankruptcy Code, it creates an "estate" to be administered by the trustee. With only the exceptions given below, the estate includes "all legal or equitable interests of the debtor in property as of the commencement of the case."

What is in that "estate"?

Although that broad language should cover everything, the law is also specific that the following types of property, which may come into existence or be recovered after the start of the case, are also property of the estate:

- If only one spouse files, and the couple has community property that is under the sole, equal, or joint management of the filing spouse, the property is probably included.
- Certain recoveries by the trustee in avoiding sales or fraudulent transfers (see part 12) are included.
- The following are included if the right to receive them occurs within 180 days of filing:

- Inherited property.
- Property settlements in divorce proceedings.
- Funds receivable as beneficiary of a life insurance policy or death-benefit plan.
- Any other interest in property that the estate acquires after filing.

Does that mean I can't keep any of my property?

Even if property is included in the estate, it may be possible to exempt it under applicable state or federal law. Exemptions are allowances that you are entitled to claim in your bankruptcy petition. They are called "exemptions" because the property you claim as exempt is property that you can keep, without regard to the distribution of your other assets to creditors in the bankruptcy proceeding. Exempt property cannot be sold by the Chapter 7 or 13 trustee for the benefit of your creditors.

When should I figure out my exemptions, and why?

Although it is possible to file your list of exemptions up to fifteen days after you file your petition, you should really know what exemptions you will be claiming before you decide to file. The nature and amount of exemptions available may affect your decision to file a petition in bankruptcy in the first place.

All right, how do exemptions work?

The types of property you may claim as exempt are governed by state and federal statutes. In some states you can only choose the state exemptions. In those states where you can take either the state or federal exemptions, the decision you make may be just as important to your economic fresh start as your decision to file for bankruptcy protection in the first place.

Is this another reason to have an attorney?

It is important to speak with your attorney about your exemptions very early in the process. The law with respect to exemptions is very complex, subject to different interpretations depending upon where you file your bankruptcy petition, and subject to change at any time. For example, the Supreme Court of the United States has just decided a very important case involving the exemption for certain kinds of retirement funds.

Another good reason to consult your attorney before choosing your exemptions is that the Chapter 7 trustee or any of your creditors may file objections to the list of property you claim as exempt. They must do this within thirty days after the conclusion of the section 341 meeting (see part 6) unless they obtain an extension of time by filing a motion within the thirty-day period.

If the trustee or a creditor objects to the exemptions you claim, they must convince the court that you are wrong — you don't have to convince the court that you are right. Your attorney can help you avoid needless and time-consuming arguments with your trustee and creditors about the validity of the exemptions you choose.

What exemptions apply to me?

The location of the Bankruptcy Court where you must file is generally within the state where you have lived for the longest time within the six months (actually, 180 days) before filing your bankruptcy petition. In the thirty-seven states on the first list below, you must use that state's bankruptcy exemptions. However, even if you must use state exemptions, you may also claim exemptions available under certain federal laws, such as:

- Foreign Service Retirement and Disability payments (22 U.S.C. section 1104);
- Social Security payments (42 U.S.C. section 407);
- Injury or death compensation payments from war-risk hazards (42 U.S.C. section 1717);
- Wages from your job as a fisherman or seaman (46 U.S.C. section 601);
- Civil Service retirement benefits (5 U.S.C. sections 729 and 2265);
- Railroad Retirement Act annuities and pensions (45 U.S.C. section 228 (L));
- Veterans' benefits (45 U.S.C. section 352 (E)); and
- Longshoremen's and Harbor Worker's Compensation Act death and disability benefits (33 U.S.C. section 916)

Your attorney will help you if any of these apply.

Where am I limited to state law exemptions?

The following states require that you choose the exemptions available to you *under state law only*:

Alabama	Idaho	Mississippi	Ohio
Alaska	Illinois	Missouri	Oklahoma
Arizona	Indiana	Montana	Oregon
Arkansas	Iowa	Nebraska	South Carolina
California	Kansas	Nevada	South Dakota
Colorado	Kentucky	New Hampshire	Tennessee
Delaware	Louisiana	New York	Utah

Florida	Maine	North Carolina	Virginia
Georgia	Maryland	North Dakota	West Virginia
			Wyoming

Appendix C sets forth in detail the property that you may claim as exempt if you live in any one of the thirty-seven states just listed. The federal exemption list is also there. The remaining states permit you to choose *either* the state or federal exemptions. These states are:

Connecticut	New Mexico
District of Columbia	Pennsylvania
Hawaii	Rhode Island
Massachusetts	Texas
Michigan	Washington
Minnesota	Wisconsin
New Jersey	Vermont

In the states that permit you to choose between the exemptions set forth in the Bankruptcy Code and those provided by state law, you must remember that you can't pick and choose. It's an all-or-nothing proposition — you can get either state or federal exemptions, not some of each.

Let's get specific; can I avoid liens that would hurt my exemption in certain property?

The Bankruptcy Code allows you to avoid certain liens that impair your exemption in specific property if you meet the appropriate tests. These liens include judicial liens resulting from judgments that may have been entered against you, as well as nonpossessory, non-purchase-money security interests in household furnishings,

wearing apparel, appliances, books, animals, crops, musical instruments, or jewelry. In order to avoid a lien on
those types of goods, you or one of your dependents
must own and use the goods for personal, family, or
household purposes. You may need to consult an attorney to understand whether or not you should file a motion to avoid any liens that impair exemptions to which
you are entitled.

And what does that mean to me?

The effect of avoiding a lien to preserve an exemption
varies considerably from court to court, and even from
judge to judge within a court. Your attorney will help
you find a way through the mine field.

Now, what is the importance of exempting property?

Property that you exempt is not normally liable for payment of any costs associated with your bankruptcy estate.
Additionally, unless your case is dismissed, property that
you exempt is not liable for any prepetition debts. Exceptions include certain tax debts, alimony and child support
obligations, debts secured by liens that you fail to avoid,
and debts owed to certain federal depository institutions
resulting from willful and malicious injuries, fraud or
misconduct while acting in a fiduciary capacity, embezzlement, or larceny. These exceptions to discharge are
discussed in part 9.

How much room to maneuver do I have?

Although you must proceed with caution, the Bankruptcy Code does not prevent you from selling nonexempt assets prior to your filing and using the proceeds ei-

ther to pay your creditors or to buy exempt assets. If you choose the first route and decide to pay unsecured creditors or a family member or friend to whom you owe money, you may have to wait to file bankruptcy for at least ninety days and perhaps as long as one year. You should read part 12 on preferences before following that route. Moreover, there is no good reason for you to pay debts that are dischargeable in bankruptcy, unless you want to maintain a relationship with a store that you use frequently to buy necessities on credit, or you want to pay a joint obligation to avoid causing a friend or relative to be saddled with paying the entire debt when you file for bankruptcy protection.

The second route, buying exempt assets, also involves some risk. If you frequently have been unemployed from your construction job and are thinking about changing your career, it may be proper for you to sell exempt "tools of your trade" and invest the proceeds in a reliable automobile that will enable you to commute to school and a part-time office job. However, if you use the proceeds to buy brand-new living room furniture and an oriental rug, you are inviting trouble down the road. You should read parts 9 and 12 on fraudulent transfers and the denial of the discharge if you are contemplating those types of transactions.

To be safe from the type of trouble such manipulations can get you into, you should be careful to sell and buy property that has approximately the same value and is reasonably priced. Avoid last-minute transfers of property before you file. Transfers made with personal greed as a motive and with the intention of defrauding creditors rarely withstand the scrutiny of competent Chapter 7 trustees and irate creditors. The filing of a Chapter 7 petition is traumatic enough without the grief you can cause yourself by improvidently trying to convert nonexempt assets into exempt assets.

So I do have some flexibility; how much exempt property do I have?

Computing the extent of your exempt property requires a multistep analysis:

1. Determine if your state allows you to take the federal exemptions. If so, perform the following steps two ways — as if you had selected the federal exemptions and as if you had picked the state statute.
2. See if you have any property of the kinds that are exempt.
3. Take the value of each piece of property, less all mortgages and unavoidable voluntary liens on it (the net value), and compare that with the maximum amount of the exemption allowed.
4. Your exemption for that item is the *lesser* of its net value and the amount of exemption allowed.

PART

12

The Trustee Can Undo Things You Have Done

Bankruptcy is intended to make sure that all creditors who hold similar claims are treated equally. For example, it is improper to pay one credit card company 100 percent of the amount due and pay only 25 percent to another credit card company.

What if I do it before I file?

Some people think that they can work those kinds of deals if they do them before they file a bankruptcy petition. However, the rules of the game generally prohibit such tactics. The trustee in bankruptcy is given special "avoiding powers." They enable him or her to undo deals and transactions that the debtor has made before the filing of the bankruptcy case.

What's the big deal?

The most common problem area involves what are called "preferential transfers," or "preferences" for short. The second involves "fraudulent conveyances," called "fraudulent transfers" in a number of states. Both transfers involve activities that violate the basic rule of fairness — one creditor is being treated better than another in the same position.

What are preferences?

There is no evil motive involved in preferences. Most are quite innocent, both as to the person who pays and the person who receives the funds, but they turn out to be preferences anyway. Basically, a preference is:

1. a transfer by an insolvent person
2. to or for the benefit of a creditor
3. made within the "preference period" (see below)
4. on account of a debt owed before the transfer was made
5. that gives the creditor who receives the transfer more than it would have received in the bankruptcy if the transfer hadn't been made. (This last will be true in virtually every case.)

How does that work?

Here is a simplified example of how the statute works:

1. Sarah has $1,000 and she owes Able $2,000 and Baker $2,000.
2. Because her liabilities exceed her assets, she is insolvent.

3. If she were in bankruptcy, the $1,000 would be divided equally between Able and Baker and each would receive $500.
4. Sarah likes Able and doesn't like Baker. So, just before she files her bankruptcy petition, she pays Able $750.
5. This is more than Able would have received if the transfer had not been made. (See the fifth part of the definition of a preference.)
6. There is now a bankruptcy in which the assets are $250, and the debts are $1,250 ($250 left owing to Able and $1,000 to Baker).
7. Unless the transfer to Able is undone, the $250 will be distributed as follows:
   A. The $250 is 20 percent of the $1,250 in total debts.
   B. Able will get 20 percent of the $250 due to him, or $50.
   C. Baker will get $200, or 20 percent of the $1,000 due to him.
8. The result of this is to give Able $800 of his $1,000 ($750 before filing and $50 after), and to give Baker only $200 of his $1,000.
9. As a result of the bankruptcy law on preferences, the trustee can make Able pay back the $750, if he can prove the elements outlined here.

As you can see, there are a number of complicated issues involved in preferences. The following explanations may clear things up a little.

First, what is a transfer?

For example, a "transfer" need not be an actual handing over of money. It could be forgiving a debt, or giving a mortgage to an existing creditor.

Second, what is insolvency?

Under the Bankruptcy Code, a person is considered insolvent if his or her debts exceed the value of his or her assets. This is called the "balance sheet" test (see part 5). There is a presumption that the debtor is insolvent during the ninety days before the filing of the petition.

Third, what is the preference period?

The time period during which the trustee can undo (the technical word is "avoid") preferences is called the "preference period." It begins to run ninety days before the filing of the petition in the normal case. However, if the person to whom the transfer is made is an "insider," the period is extended to a full year. The presumption of insolvency is not extended, so that a trustee must prove insolvency when going against an insider on transfers made more than ninety days before the filing.

Who are those "insiders"?

You don't have to be very close to be an "insider" as that term is used in the Bankruptcy Code. The definition includes relatives "related by affinity or consanguinity within the third degree as determined by the common law," as well as "step" relations or adopted persons falling into those classes. Relationships within that degree are parents, grandparents, great-grandparents, and uncles and aunts, looking at ancestors, and the parallel relationships, looking at descendants.

The term "insider" also includes a partnership in which the debtor is a general partner, or a corporation in which the debtor is a director, officer, or person in control.

Are there other insiders I should know about?

In many bankruptcy courts, a creditor completely unrelated to the debtor may be considered an insider if the debt is guaranteed by a person or entity that is itself an insider. This is a very complicated area of the law, and some courts do not agree with the concept. Your lawyer will be able to tell you the status of the issue in the court where the bankruptcy is or will be pending.

So I have to be careful; are there any loopholes?

There are certain limited exceptions to the preference rules. The primary ones of interest to individuals are these:

1. Payments made in the ordinary course of the financial affairs of the debtor, such as regular monthly payments on charge accounts or loans, are not preferential even if they satisfy all of the tests.
2. If the debtor's obligations are primarily consumer debts, transfers under $600 are exempt.

I think I understand preferences; what about fraudulent transfers?

The notion of fraudulent transfers dates back to a statute entitled "Statute Against Fraudulent Deeds, Alienations, Etc.," which was adopted in the thirteenth year of the reign of the first Queen Elizabeth (1570). The concept covers a broad variety of conduct. The basic question then and now is this: has the debtor disposed of an asset for less than it was worth?

Three phrases are used interchangeably by lawyers: "the Statute of Elizabeth" (becoming obsolete), "fraudulent conveyances," and "fraudulent transfers." The first comes from the 1570 law just mentioned. The latter two arise from state statutes on the subject. Most states adopted the Uniform Fraudulent Conveyances Act (UFCA for short). The UFCA is being replaced in an increasing number of states by the Uniform Fraudulent Transfers Act (UFTA). In addition to rights under the Statute of Elizabeth, UFCA, or UFTA, whichever is the law of the applicable state, a bankruptcy trustee also has powers under section 548 of the Bankruptcy Code.

If the trustee's going to get me, does it make any difference whether it's under state or federal law?

The big difference between the state and federal laws is the "statute of limitations." Under section 548, the questioned transfer must have occurred within the year before the filing of the petition. State statutes vary, but most look at transfers much further back.

If you suspect a fraudulent transfer, first look for a "transfer," which may be a sale, gift, mortgage, or other transaction, and see if it happened within the time period specified by the Bankruptcy Code or state law. If it has, you look for one of two kinds of fact patterns.

What is the most common pattern of facts?

The first type of activity, called "common-law fraud" by lawyers, has given rise to fraudulent transfer claims for centuries. It requires the following:

1. The debtor either made a transfer or incurred an obligation during the statutory period; and
2. The debtor acted with an intent to hinder, delay, or defraud his or her creditors.

We'll call the first part a "transfer" to make reading easier, but you should remember that it includes incurring an obligation, like granting a mortgage.

The second part, and in particular the "intent" aspect, is the hard part. Sometimes it is very difficult to determine what was in a person's mind when a transfer was made. Over the centuries, certain kinds of conduct have proven to be such persuasive evidence of fraudulent intent that they are called "badges of fraud." Badges of fraud may be used to help prove intent. They include:

- A close relationship between the debtor and the person to whom the transfer is made.
- The retention of possession or use of property despite its transfer, just as if the property had never been transferred.
- Attempts to keep the transfer secret.
- The debtor's receipt of less than full value for the property.
- The falsity of a deed or bill of sale stating that the debtor received full value for the transfer when actually little value or nothing at all was received.

What if I'm just a lousy negotiator and got less than full value for that reason?

Even though a transfer for less than full value is one of the badges of fraud, evidence of intent must still be proven to make a case of common-law fraud. Section 548 and many state statutes provide an easier route for the trustee who is trying to undo a transaction.

Starting with a transfer for less than full value, *one of the following facts* must be added:

- The debtor was insolvent (see discussion earlier in this chapter) at the time the transfer was made; *or*
- The debtor had been solvent, but the effect of the transfer was to make the debtor insolvent; *or*
- The debtor was engaged in business, or about to start a business, and the transfer left the debtor with unreasonably small capital; *or*
- The debtor intended to or believed that he would incur debts beyond his ability to pay.

If the trustee can prove any one of those necessary facts, along with the debtor's receipt of less than full value for the property transferred, the deal can be undone.

WARNING: The Official Forms require the debtor to disclose all extraordinary transfers during the year immediately before the filing of the petition. The purpose of the requirement is to reveal information that may lead to recovery of preferences or fraudulent transfers. Failure to report such a transaction might result in a denial of a discharge in a Chapter 7 case or dismissal or conversion of a Chapter 13 case.

PART

13

Keeping Property After Bankruptcy

If you file for bankruptcy protection owing property, you must list the property and determine if each item is subject to or free of liens. You'll generally know this without much trouble — if you bought a car and agreed to pay $300 each month until the price was paid, you'll probably find a lien on your motor vehicle title naming the bank or other financier to whom you make payments.

What other situations might produce liens?

If you have borrowed to refinance debts, you may have to check through your paperwork to see if the new financier took the property that was refinanced as collateral for the new loan.

In the case of real estate, you know if you have a mortgage on your property. Additionally, if you have been sued, it is possible that the person suing you obtained an attachment or a judgment that became a lien on your property.

How will anyone know what I've got?

One of the forms that is filed at the time of a bankruptcy petition (it can be filed a little later, but almost no one takes that option) is Form 8: the Statement of Intention. You'll find a copy at the end of the book. On it you list all property that secures consumer debts and what you intend to do with the property. You have two basic options: surrender the property to the creditor or keep it. The Bankruptcy Code defines a "consumer debt" as a "debt incurred by an individual primarily for a personal, family, or household purpose."

How do I go about surrendering property?

If you wish to surrender the property, you simply list it in section 2 of the form. You are supposed to return it to the creditor within forty-five days, but most lawyers feel that it is up to the creditor to make arrangements for the return. Selection of this option frees you from the debt to the extent of the value of the property. The remainder, if any, will be discharged in a Chapter 7 proceeding (a non-dischargeable debt of this type would be rare, but it is possible) or paid as an unsecured debt under the plan in Chapter 13.

And if I want to keep it?

There are three techniques for retaining property:

1. reaffirming the obligation to pay for the property;

2. claiming the property as exempt and redeeming it; and

3. claiming the property as exempt and avoiding liens on it.

Why should I reaffirm a debt when I'm trying to get my debts discharged?

Suppose you owe $3,000 on a car that is not worth that much. You may wish to keep the car and structure an agreement with the creditor so that you can continue to make payments as if there had been no bankruptcy. That is called "reaffirmation" under the Bankruptcy Code. It should be very simple, but it isn't.

Why? The statute itself is a bit mixed up because of some amendments. It's as if you put a Ford muffler on a Cadillac — you're not really sure if it's going to do the job. Lawyers and courts differ on what the law means, and how it works.

For example, if your car is only worth $4,000 and you want to keep it, even if it means reaffirming an $8,000 debt, many judges will not approve the reaffirmation agreement. Under those circumstances, and especially if there will not be any dividend to the creditor beyond the value of the car, the creditor may be willing to reduce the amount of its claim as part of the reaffirmation agreement.

Is reaffirmation another area it takes a lawyer to sort out?

The following discussion gives a conservative view of what you can do, but your lawyer (and you really need one in this area) will know what the local judges will permit — some may be more liberal.

You should enter into a reaffirmation agreement with your creditor quickly. In most courts it must be filed within forty-five days of your original bankruptcy filing. A statement of the amount owed and the value of the collateral, if any, as well as the creditor's agreement and signature are necessary, as shown on Form B240, which follows this chapter. That form is not required so long as the document you do use contains all of the points covered in the official form.

CAUTION: Some creditors will send a representative to the section 341 meeting (discussed in part 6) who will try to persuade you to reaffirm a debt. You should never reaffirm a debt unless you know exactly what you are doing. Ask your attorney for advice on the particular contract that you are thinking about reaffirming.

If you have a lawyer, the lawyer will explain the nature of the agreement to you and sign the form, indicating that he or she has provided the explanation. The lawyer must also certify that the reaffirmation does not impose an undue hardship on you or your dependents. If you do not have a lawyer, you will have to convince the judge that the agreement is in your best interest. Part C of Form B240 is an example of the kind of information required.

What if I don't have a lawyer?

If you do not have a lawyer, some judges will require you to come to court so that they can be sure that you understand what you are doing. Some will require you to come

to court even if your lawyer certifies that he has explained things to you.

Can I reaffirm my way into keeping my plastic?

People sometimes want to use reaffirmation agreements
to keep credit cards. That is, they are willing to continue
payments on the card in order to keep the card. No property is involved. Many judges will not permit a debtor to
do that, or will only permit it if some very good reason
can be shown. Your lawyer will be the best guide as to
what is permitted in a particular court.

Am I stuck if I reaffirm and realize I was stupid to do so?

If you have signed a reaffirmation agreement and later
change your mind, you can get out of the agreement, but
only within sixty days of the time that the agreement is
filed in court or at any time prior to discharge, whichever is later.

You said if I didn't reaffirm I could redeem exempt property; what does that mean?

In part 12 you were able to determine that items of your
property are exempt under the laws, federal or state, applicable to the place where you would file a bankruptcy
petition. To the extent that there is a lien on such property, and that property is tangible personal property intended primarily for personal, family, or household use,
it can be redeemed by paying the creditor the present
value of the property within forty-five days.

You can also redeem that kind of property if it is abandoned by the trustee.

Notice that it is only the present value of the property that must be paid. Even if you owe more, you get to pay off the lien at the present value of the property. After all, that is all that the creditor would get if you surrendered the item.

Is that as good a deal as it sounds?

The difficulty with this option is that you have to pay cash within forty-five days. Also, you have to agree with the creditor on the value of the property, although that seldom appears to be a problem.

The third choice you mentioned, "lien avoidance on exempt property," sounds complex; what is it?

"Lien avoidance" is a technique under the Bankruptcy Code to preserve the value of exemptions. It is highly technical and subject to many conflicting court decisions.

First, the property must have value over and above all consensual liens, such as mortgages and purchase-money security interests. Next, the property must be of the kind in which you can claim an exemption. (Exemptions are discussed in part 11.)

Judicial liens can be "avoided" in *any* exempt property. Nonpossessory, non–purchase-money security interests can be avoided only in

1. household furnishings, household goods, wearing apparel, appliances, books, animals, crops, musical instruments, or jewelry that is held primarily for the personal, family, or household use of the debtor or a dependent of the debtor;

2. implements, professional books, or tools of the trade of the debtor or the trade of a dependent of the debtor; or

3. professionally prescribed health aids for the debtor or a dependent of the debtor.

Do you have a simplified example of this one?

Here's an example of a somewhat simple case:

John's house is exempt-type propertyand is now worth	$200,000.
John owes a mortgage on the house of	(150,000).
If that were all, John's exemption would come out of the	$ 50,000.
BUT there is a judgment lien on the house of	(50,000).
which eats up the equity, leaving the exemption at	0.

This is an obvious case where John's exemption (which we'll say is $7,500) is wiped out by the judicial lien. That situation is not permitted, but how it is handled varies from judge to judge.

Some judges would wipe out the entire judicial lien, since it interferes with the exemption. The effect of that would be to give John's bankruptcy estate $42,500, not $7,500, if the Chapter 7 trustee should sell the property at its present value. Other judges would simply reduce the judicial lien to $42,500, which results in John's having his $7,500 exemption preserved. Still other judges would say that, on a sale of the property, John must get

$7,500 before the holder of the judgment lien gets anything, but the lien remains in place.

Consult your attorney for the views in your court.

You said it was complex; are those three methods the only ways I can keep property?

The Bankruptcy Code specifically permits you to make arrangements with the holder of a security interest outside of the bankruptcy case. For example, you and your creditor might agree that you can keep the property so long as you keep up the monthly payments.

Most lawyers and courts have the opinion that your personal liability for the debt has been wiped out by the bankruptcy, and all that the secured creditor has is the lien on the property. Under that view, the worst thing that can happen is that the property will be repossessed at some time in the future. However, there is at least one decision that says that failure to use one of the three techniques in the Bankruptcy Code preserves personal liability on these facts. If there is not a binding decision in your jurisdiction, the informal route can be a most dangerous one.

Keeping Property After Bankruptcy

B 240 (1/88)	REAFFIRMATION AGREEMENT	
Debtor's Name		Bankruptcy Case No.

INSTRUCTIONS:

1) Write debtor's name and bankruptcy case number above.
2) Part A — Must be signed by both the debtor and the creditor.
3) Part B — Must be signed by the attorney who represents the debtor in this bankruptcy case.
4) Part C — Must be completed by the debtor if the debtor is not represented by an attorney in this bankruptcy case.
5) File the completed form by mailing or delivering to the Bankruptcy Clerk.
6) Attach written agreement, if any.

COURT USE ONLY

PART A — AGREEMENT

Creditor's Name and Address

Summary of Terms of the New Agreement

a) Principal Amount $ _____
   Interest Rate (APR) _____
   Monthly Payments $ _____
b) Description of Security: _____

Date Set for Discharge Hearing (If any)

Present Market Value $ _____

The parties understand that this agreement is purely voluntary and that the debtor may rescind the agreement at any time prior to discharge or within 60 days after such agreement is filed with the court, whichever occurs later, by giving notice of rescission to the creditor.

_____ _____
Date   Signature of Debtor

_____ _____
Signature of Creditor   Signature of Joint Debtor

PART B — ATTORNEY'S DECLARATION

This agreement represents a fully informed and voluntary agreement that does not impose an undue hardship on the debtor or any dependent of the debtor.

_____ _____
Date   Signature of Debtor's Attorney

PART C — MOTION FOR COURT APPROVAL OF AGREEMENT — Complete only where debtor is not represented by an attorney.

I (we), the debtor, affirm the following to be true and correct:

1) I am not represented by an attorney in connection with this bankruptcy case.
2) My current monthly net income is $ _____
3) My current monthly expenses total $ _____, including any payment due under this agreement.
4) I believe that this agreement is in my best interest because _____

Therefore, I ask the court for an order approving this reaffirmation agreement.

_____ _____
Date   Signature of Debtor

_____
Signature of Joint Debtor

PART D — COURT ORDER

The court grants the debtor's motion and approves the voluntary agreement upon the terms specified above.

_____ _____
Date   Bankruptcy Judge

PART

14

Information for Creditors

This chapter is designed for the benefit of persons who are owed money by (including landlords of) persons who file for protection under the Bankruptcy Code. If you are not familiar with the bankruptcy system, you might wish to read quickly through parts 2 (How the Bankruptcy Law Works), 6 (How Chapter 7 Works), and 7 (How Chapter 13 Works), before going on.

Remember that this book does not cover Chapter 11, the reorganization chapter of the Bankruptcy Code, used by many businesses and some individuals with substantial debts as an alternative to liquidation under Chapter 7 or adjustment of debts under Chapter 13. This discussion will be about creditors' rights in cases under Chapters 7 and 13 involving individual debtors and married couples.

These two examples illustrate typical situations involving creditors and debtors:

Case No. 1 Jane owes you money. You have just received a notice from the United States Bankruptcy Court that she has filed for protection under the Bankruptcy Code. How are your rights affected as a creditor? What can you do to collect your money?

Case No. 2 Dick is a tenant in an apartment house that you own. He is months behind in his rent, and you have started an action in the state court to evict him. You receive notice from the Bankruptcy Court that Dick has filed for protection under the Bankruptcy Code. Can you continue with the eviction action? Can you collect the back rent?

The answers to the questions posed will become clear from the discussion that follows.

THE AUTOMATIC STAY

In both of the sample cases your collection or eviction efforts must come to a complete and immediate stop. You are faced with the "automatic stay," which prevents collection or eviction action without permission of the Bankruptcy Court. The automatic stay arises without any action on anyone's part. The filing of the bankruptcy petition itself creates the stay. The filing operates as a stay of virtually any action you would like to take to collect the money due to you.

There are exceptions in the statute, but none apply in either of the cases given here. Exceptions to the operation of the automatic stay are discussed in part 6, where you will find the text of the statute.

A creditor who attempts to take or takes action in violation of the automatic stay is in contempt of court. Most bankruptcy judges will take action to protect the debtor from violations or will issue sanctions against creditors who have violated the stay. Should you give up? Should you write off the debt? Should you let a nonpaying tenant remain in your property? No! There may be things you can do that are specifically authorized by the Bankruptcy Code.

The nature of your rights in bankruptcy proceedings depends upon whether your claim is secured or unsecured, and the chapter under which the debtor filed. If your claim is secured, there may be differences depending upon the nature of the collateral.

THE UNSECURED CREDITOR

Proof of Claim

Chapter 7

Take a good look at the notice you received from the Bankruptcy Court. It will tell you under which chapter the debtor filed. It also contains most of the information you need to exercise your rights.

The first step is to look for a "no-asset" statement in the notice. Official Form B9A reads like this:

Caption: NOTICE OF COMMENCEMENT OF CASE UNDER CHAPTER 7 OF THE BANKRUPTCY

CODE, MEETING OF CREDITORS AND FIXING OF DATES (*Individual or Joint Debtor No-Asset Case*)

In Body: AT THIS TIME THERE APPEAR TO BE NO ASSETS AVAILABLE FROM WHICH PAYMENT MAY BE MADE TO UNSECURED CREDITORS. DO NOT FILE A PROOF OF CLAIM UNTIL YOU RECEIVE NOTICE TO DO SO.

Above Signature Block: DO NOT FILE A PROOF OF CLAIM UNLESS YOU RECEIVE A COURT NOTICE TO DO SO.

The net effect of all this language is to tell you that the debtor has filed schedules indicating that there are no free assets that could be sold to pay unsecured creditors' claims. This may be because there actually are no assets or because the assets that do exist are exempt (see part 11).

Whether you will do anything after you receive such a notice is your decision. If you do not want to question or challenge the "no-asset" status of the case, just charge off the debt and forget about it. You'll most likely never see your money.

If the schedules filed with the court indicate that there may be some assets available for distribution to creditors, in most courts you won't see the "no-asset" language in the notice you receive from the Bankruptcy Court. Instead, it will tell you, in the words of Official Form B9C,

> Except as otherwise provided by law, in order to share in any payment from the estate, a creditor must file a proof of claim by the date set forth above in the box labelled "Filing Claims." The place to file the proof of claim, either in person or by mail, is the office of the

clerk of the bankruptcy court. Proof of claim forms are available in the clerk's office of any bankruptcy court.

A copy of Official Form 10, the official proof of claim form, is reproduced at the end of this chapter. It is fairly easy to complete.

Be sure that you file your proof of claim as soon as possible. Obtain a time-stamped copy by enclosing a duplicate of your claim and a stamped, self-addressed envelope for the return. The proof of claim should set forth the amount of money you are owed for goods sold, rent, a loan, or whatever. If the claim arises from a promissory note, lease, or other document, a copy of the document should be attached to the court's copy of the proof of claim. An indication of how you arrived at the amount due, such as a copy of the account history or a statement showing account activity and the balance due, should be attached. These steps can save you a substantial amount of time in your dealings with the trustee in a Chapter 7 case or the debtor and his or her attorney in a Chapter 13 case.

Chapter 13

If the case has been filed under Chapter 13, the notice will tell you so. It also may be accompanied by a copy of the debtor's plan, or will tell you that you will receive it later. It will also give you dates for the filing of your proof of claim, and the date, time, and place of the meeting of creditors. In a Chapter 13 case, you must file your proof of claim by the deadline set out in the notice you receive from the court. This will allow the debtor to provide for your claim in his or her Chapter 13 plan (see part 8).

Unlike those in Chapter 7, the provisions for the discharge in Chapter 13 are very broad, and the circumstances under which your claim might be exempted from discharge quite narrow. Thus, the only way you may obtain any recovery on your claim is through the debtor's plan.

The Meeting of Creditors

If you think that there is something "fishy" going on, or you just want more information about the debtor's situation, you may want to attend the meeting of creditors. You can go yourself; you don't need a lawyer for that purpose.

The date, time, and place of the meeting are also in the notice you received. It is called a "341 meeting," after the number of the section of the Bankruptcy Code that requires it to be held.

The debtor must appear at that meeting and "submit to examination under oath." You will be able to question the debtor about his or her affairs and property. If no creditor is interested in the debtor's affairs, the meeting will be over in a few minutes.

If you plan to attend the meeting, it is advisable to go to the court before the date of the hearing and examine the papers filed by the debtor. Information about the debtor's financial affairs should be on the Official Forms, copies of which are at the back of this book in appendix A.

It is possible that a debtor may not have filed schedules with the original petition, and may even have obtained court permission to file them later, perhaps even beyond the date of the section 341 meeting. If you suspect a real problem, you might want to ask — at the meeting — that it be continued to a date in the future after the debtor has filed the schedules and you have had an opportunity to review them. (Most bankruptcy courts have procedures to dismiss cases automatically when the schedules are not filed on time.)

The forms should contain a list all of the debtor's assets, liabilities, and claimed exemptions. They will give you a starting point for questioning the debtor. For example, if the debtor claims to own a 1978 Ford, and you happen to know he is driving around in a 1988 Cadillac, you might want to ask appropriate questions.

Also, if you suspect that the debtor improperly claimed property as exempt, you may want to ask appropriate questions and, if necessary, file an objection. An objection to property claimed to be exempt must be filed within thirty days of the conclusion of the section 341 meeting.

Filing false schedules is a crime, although it is seldom prosecuted except in the most serious cases.

Discharge and Dischargeability

If you feel that something is seriously wrong, you should talk to the Chapter 7 or Chapter 13 trustee or the United States Trustee. If the dollars justify it, this is the time to hire an attorney.

Given the right facts, in a Chapter 7 case, you might file a complaint objecting either to the dischargeability of your claim or to the debtor's discharge in general. (Dischargeability issues are quite different in Chapter 13; see part 7.)

Those matters are discussed in detail in part 9, but, for present purposes, you should know that a debtor may be denied discharge of *all* debts if he or she has committed any of these acts:

- Fraudulent transfer, concealment, or destruction of property.
- Failure to keep records, or destruction of records.
- False oath or claim in connection with the bankruptcy case.
- Bribery in connection with the bankruptcy case.
- Failure to cooperate with the trustee (of course, this occurs later in the case).
- Failure to explain loss of assets.
- Failure to obey lawful orders of the bankruptcy court.
- Committing certain acts like these in a related bankruptcy case.

Dischargeability, on the other hand, relates to a particular debt. The loose classifications of events that could result in nondischargeability of a claim in a Chapter 7 case include:

- Fraudulently incurring the debt.
- Failing to schedule debts.
- Acting fraudulently in a fiduciary capacity.
- Committing willful and malicious acts.

In addition, certain classes of obligations are simply not dischargeable because of how they arose. These include certain taxes, alimony, and child support obligations. Part 9 contains a detailed discussion of discharge and dischargeability litigation.

It is to your advantage to have a debtor freed from all or most of his or her other obligations and still owing you after the conclusion of the bankruptcy proceeding.

If the notice indicates that there are no assets, you can still review the schedules and attend the meeting of creditors, if you feel that there might be something to gain, just as in the case of a "asset" notice.

Regardless of your decision to object to either the debtor's discharge or the dischargeability of your claim, the property of the estate will be administered by the Chapter 7 trustee, as described in part 6.

THE SECURED CREDITOR

Secured creditors also receive the same type of notice from the bankruptcy court. However, since they have some security for the obligation the debtor owes them, and the automatic stay prevents actions to repossess, sell, or otherwise act in connection with the collateral, such creditors will want to do more than the unsecured creditors described in the earlier part of this discussion. They will want to get their hands on the security, or, if they already have it, get permission to dispose of it.

The first step might be to ask the debtor (preferably through his or her attorney) if the debtor wishes to keep the collateral and continue making the payments. If the debtor agrees, you can enter into a reaffirmation agreement, which must be approved by the bankruptcy judge. This procedure, described in more detail in part 13, must be done early in the case. The best place to explore the possibility of reaching a reaffirmation agreement is at the section 341 meeting. "Professional" creditors have preprinted forms that they bring with them. Considering that many of the forms those people use don't pass muster with stricter judges, you are probably better off just using Official Form B240, a copy of which is at the end of part 13. That part also has more detailed information on reaffirmation.

If the debtor has no equity in the property — that is, the amount owed to you and other creditors and secured by the collateral exceeds the value of the collateral — the debtor may be willing to turn the collateral over to you and walk away. This can also be done by agreement. The trustee may also agree to abandon the property. In some circumstances you may even ask the court to compel the trustee to abandon the property.

The more difficult situation is when the debtor wishes to keep the property, either permanently or just to stall as long as possible. You must now apply to the Bankruptcy Court for help.

The technique used is called a "motion for relief from stay" and experienced attorneys who represent creditors in bankruptcy cases have the basic form in their computers. There is no standard nationwide form, as local rules in the various bankruptcy courts set forth differing requirements.

Motion for Relief from Stay

In a Chapter 7 case, success on the motion will depend upon whether there is value in the property over and above all mortgages, liens, and property taxes. If there is, the trustee will want a chance to sell the property in the usual way rather than allowing you to foreclose and repossess.

Foreclosure is a "forced sale" that usually results in the receipt of less than fair market value for the property sold, a situation that is detrimental to the debtor, other secured creditors, and unsecured creditors. If the values of sale by the trustee and a forced sale are close, the trustee may agree to giving the property back to you to sell provided that you sell "in a commercially reasonable manner," account to the trustee for the results of the sale, and turn over proceeds in excess of your secured claim, if any. If there is clearly no equity, your motion probably will be granted.

Your attorney — you'll need one to file such a motion properly — can explain the further ramifications. Since the filing fee for a motion for relief from stay is $60, you will want to make sure the motion is properly prepared and the appropriate notice given.

In a Chapter 13 case, the debtor can resist the motion for relief from stay by demonstrating that the property is necessary for his or her plan of reorganization, and that the plan is feasible. Check with your attorney on how much weight this carries with the judges in the bankruptcy court where the petition is pending.

If you are a landlord, you may also be in a position to file a motion for relief from stay. Essentially, you will be asking the court for permission to proceed in the state court to evict the debtor from your property. This is a separate remedy from collecting the amount of back rent the debtor may owe you. That amount is an unsecured claim for which you should file a proof of claim as described earlier in this part.

Success on your motion will depend on a variety of factors. If your lease with the debtor expired before the bankruptcy petition was filed, or it was terminated because of defaults by the debtor, you will likely obtain relief from the stay. However, if the debtor is current in his or her rental obligations, you will not be in a position to obtain court authority to proceed with an eviction simply because of the bankruptcy filing.

If the debtor has paid his or her rent under a lease before the filing of the petition, but has failed to pay you after the filing, you may need to file a different type of motion — one to compel the assumption or rejection of the lease and the payment of what is known as an administrative claim. You should consult an attorney in this situation, as the law and the calculation of your claim are more complex.

INVOLUNTARY PETITIONS

If you are owed money by someone who has not filed a bankruptcy petition, but you think that a trustee could undo some detrimental things that the debtor has done (see part 13), you might consider filing an involuntary Chapter 7 petition. You cannot file an involuntary Chapter 13 petition (and we are not discussing Chapter 11, where involuntary petitions are also permitted, in this book).

Involuntary petitions normally require the signatures of three creditors with undisputed claims totalling at least $5,000. If there are fewer than twelve creditors, only one signature is needed on the petition. That means, in the normal case, you will be scurrying around to find two more creditors.

The repercussions to you for filing an improper involuntary petition can be severe, and may include punitive damages for an improper filing. If you are thinking this way, consult a bankruptcy attorney specializing in creditors' rights before you say anything to anyone.

PERSONAL BANKRUPTCY

FORM B10
(6/90)

FORM 10. PROOF OF CLAIM

United States Bankruptcy Court _____ District of _____	PROOF OF CLAIM
In re (Name of Debtor)	Case Number

NOTE: This form should not be used to make a claim for an administrative expense arising after the commencement of the case. A "request" of payment of an administrative expense may be filed pursuant to 11 U.S.C § 503.

Name of Creditor *(The person or entity to whom the debtor owes money or property)*	☐ Check box if you are aware that anyone else has filed a proof of claim relating to your claim. Attach copy of statement giving particulars.	
Name and Addresses Where Notices Should be Sent	☐ Check box if you have never received any notices from the bankruptcy court in this case.	
	☐ Check box if the address differs from the address on the envelope sent to you by the court.	THIS SPACE IS FOR COURT USE ONLY
Telephone No.		

ACCOUNT OR OTHER NUMBER BY WHICH CREDITOR IDENTIFIES DEBTOR: Check here if this claim ☐ replaces } a previously filed claim, dated: _____ ☐ amends

1. BASIS FOR CLAIM

☐ Goods sold
☐ Services performed
☐ Money loaned
☐ Personal injury/wrongful death
☐ Taxes
☐ Other (Describe briefly)

☐ Retiree benefits as defined in 11 U.S.C. § 1114(a)
☐ Wages, salaries, and compensations (Fill out below)
Your social security number _____
Unpaid compensations for services performed
from _____ to _____
　　　(date)　　　　　　　　　(date)

2. DATE DEBT WAS INCURRED	3. IF COURT JUDGMENT, DATE OBTAINED:

4. CLASSIFICATION OF CLAIM. Under the Bankruptcy Code all claims are classified as one or more of the following: (1) Unsecured nonpriority, (2) Unsecured Priority, (3) Secured. It is possible for part of a claim to be in one category and part in another. CHECK THE APPROPRIATE BOX OR BOXES that best describe your claim and STATE THE AMOUNT OF THE CLAIM.

☐ SECURED CLAIM $ _____
Attach evidence of perfection of security interest
Brief Description of Collateral:
☐ Real Estate ☐ Motor Vehicle ☐ Other (Describe briefly)

Amount of arrearage and other charges included in secured claim above. if any $ _____

☐ UNSECURED NONPRIORITY CLAIM $ _____
A claim is unsecured if there is no collateral or lien on property of the debtor securing the claim or to the extent that the value of such property is less than the amount of the claim.

☐ UNSECURED PRIORITY CLAIM $ _____
Specify the priority of the claim.
☐ Wages, salaries, or commissions (up to $ 2000), earned not more than 90 days before filing of the bankruptcy petition or cessation of the debtor's business, whichever is earlier) - 11 U.S.C. § 507(a)(3)
☐ Contributions to an employee benefit plan - U.S.C. § 507(a)(4)
☐ Up to $ 900 of deposits toward purchase, lease, or rental of property or services for personal, family, or household use - 11 U.S.C. § 507(a)(6)
☐ Taxes or penalties of governmental units - 11 U.S.C. § 507(a)(7)
☐ Other - 11 U.S.C. §§ 507(a)(2), (a)(5) - (Describe briefly)

5. TOTAL AMOUNT OF CLAIM AT TIME CASE FILED:	$ _____ (Unsecured)	$ _____ (Secured)	$ _____ (Priority)	$ _____ (Total)

☐ Check this box if claim includes prepetition charges in addition to the principal amount of the claim. Attach itemized statement of all additional charges.

6. CREDITS AND SETOFFS: The amount of all payments on this claim has been credited and deducted for the purpose of making this proof of claim. In filing this claim, claimant has deducted all amounts that claimant owes to debtor.   THIS SPACE IS FOR COURT USE ONLY

7. SUPPORTING DOCUMENTS: Attach copies of supporting documents, such as promissory notes, purchase orders, invoices, itemized statements of running accounts, contracts, court judgments, or evidence of security interests. If the documents are not available, explain. If the documents are voluminous, attach a summary.

8. TIME-STAMPED COPY: To receive an acknowledgment of the filing of your claim, enclose a stamped, self-addressed envelope and copy of this proof of claim.

Date	Sign and print the name and title, if any, of the creditor or other person authorized to file this claim (attach copy of power of attorney, if any)

Penalty for presenting fraudulent claim: Fine of up to $500,000 or imprisonment for up to 5 years, or both. 18 U.S.C. §§ 152 and 3571.

FPI-RBK-6/91

128

PART

15

Information for Guarantors and Co-Signers

For bankruptcy purposes there is no real difference between a guarantor and a co-signer (often called a co-maker). The former probably signed a separate piece of paper; the latter just added his or her name to a note or other credit arrangement. As far as we are concerned here, both are people who agreed to be responsible for the debts or obligations of someone else and that someone else is now in bankruptcy! We'll call both guarantors and co-signers "co-debtors" for purposes of this discussion.

If you are the person concerned about such a situation, let us look at where you are.

If the debtor—the person for whom you are co-debtor—has filed for protection under Chapter 7, the automatic stay protects the debtor from creditor action. You can read about that in detail in part 6. But that protection does not extend to you. The debtor cannot be sued; you can.

There are some extraordinary circumstances where the bankruptcy court will protect a co-debtor in a different person's bankruptcy case, but in the normal situation those circumstances do not exist.

Depending upon the pressure being exerted by the creditor and the amount of the obligation, it may well be time for you to consult an attorney for yourself.

The situation in Chapter 13 may be a bit better. Chapter 13 has a special provision that is designed to protect you to some extent, in some cases.

Under Chapter 13, the automatic stay applies to prevent collection efforts against individuals who have obligated themselves on *consumer debts* incurred for the benefit of someone else. The purpose of this is to protect the debtor from pressure that you, a friend, or relative may bring to force the debtor to get you off the hook.

The stay that applies to co-debtors, commonly called "the co-debtor stay," operates to prevent action only against individuals and then only with respect to debts incurred by the debtor primarily for personal, family, or household purposes. It does not apply if the Chapter 13 case is closed, dismissed, or converted to another chapter of the Bankruptcy Code.

The co-debtor stay continues in effect until the debtor's Chapter 13 case is closed, dismissed, or converted, unless the stay is modified or terminated by the court. As you will see, the court will often "lift the stay."

There are three grounds for relief from the co-debtor stay:

1. The debtor did not receive the consideration for the claim. That is, the co-debtor received the benefit of the transaction.
2. The debtor's Chapter 13 plan does not propose to pay the creditor's claim in full (including the payment of postpetition interest). Under these circumstances, the creditor may obtain relief from the stay to pursue the co-debtor to the extent that the debt will not be repaid.
3. The interests of the creditor would be irreparably harmed by the continuation of the stay. Examples of such harm include the filing of a bankruptcy petition by the co-debtor, financial problems encountered by the co-debtor, and the likelihood that the co-debtor will move and the creditor will be unable to commence a lawsuit against the co-debtor to satisfy the obligation.

In order to obtain relief from the co-debtor stay, the creditor must file a motion setting forth the grounds for relief. If the creditor alleges that the debtor's plan does not propose to pay the claim in full, the motion will be allowed and the creditor will obtain relief from the stay at the expiration of twenty days, *unless* the debtor or co-debtor objects, in which case a hearing will be scheduled. If the creditor alleges other grounds, the stay will not be automatically lifted without notice and a hearing. Notice of the hearing must be given to the debtor, the Chapter 13 trustee, other parties in interest, and the co-debtor.

It is often difficult for the court to determine the extent to which a plan proposes to pay a claim. Many courts have determined that a creditor is entitled to relief from the co-debtor stay if the plan fails to provide for postpetition interest, since the interest continues to accrue on the claim and is collectable from the co-debtor. However, other courts have reasoned that since postpetition interest is not allowable on unsecured and undersecured claims, failure to provide for such interest is not grounds for relief from the co-debtor stay, although the creditor would be able to collect the interest from the co-debtor at the end of the Chapter 13 case.

PART

16

Bankruptcy Crimes

Certain activities by a debtor can have unpleasant *civil* consequences. For example, a claim may not be dischargeable or payments made may be recovered for the benefit of the estate. However, those situations create only monetary problems, and while they can be bad, they cannot result in a jail sentence.

Are there some activities that will result in a fine or jail?

Other kinds of actions have more serious results — they are crimes under federal law. Debtors as well as nondebtors, either acting together or separately, can be prosecuted for these actions.

The following offenses carry a penalty of a fine up to $5,000 or imprisonment for not more than five years:

- Knowingly and fraudulently concealing property of the estate, or records relating to the property or financial affairs of a debtor, from a trustee.

- Making a false oath or account in connection with a bankruptcy case.
- Presenting a false claim against an estate.
- Knowingly and willfully receiving any material amount of property from a debtor after a petition is filed, with intent to defeat the provisions of the Bankruptcy Code.
- Knowingly and fraudulently giving, receiving, or attempting a bribe for acting or forbearing to act in a bankruptcy case.
- Knowingly and fraudulently concealing, destroying, mutilating, or falsifying books and records relating to the property or financial affairs of the debtor, either after a case is filed or in contemplation of filing.
- Entering into an agreement to fix the fees to be paid from the estate.

Do they ever go after anyone for those crimes?

Even a hint of criminal conduct in a bankruptcy case will cause the creditors, the trustee, and the court to begin a close examination of the affairs of the debtor. In appropriate cases, federal law enforcement authorities will be involved.

Appendix A

OFFICIAL BANKRUPTCY FORMS

Appendix A

FORM B1
(6/90)

FORM 1. VOLUNTARY PETITION

United States Bankruptcy Court District of _____	VOLUNTARY PETITION

IN RE (Name of debtor - If individual, enter Last, First, Middle)	NAME OF JOINT DEBTOR (Spouse) (Last, First, Middle)
ALL OTHER NAMES used by the debtor in the last 6 years (Include married, maiden, and trade names)	ALL OTHER NAMES used by the joint debtor in the last 6 years (Include married, maiden, and trade names)
SOC. SEC./TAX I.D. NO. (If more than one, state all)	SOC. SEC. TAX/I.D. NO. (If more than one, state all)
STREET ADDRESS OF DEBTOR (No. and street, city, state, and zip code)	STREET ADDRESS OF JOINT DEBTOR (No. and street, city, state, and zip code)
COUNTY OF RESIDENCE OR PRINCIPAL PLACE OF BUSINESS	COUNTY OF RESIDENCE OR PRINCIPAL PLACE OF BUSINESS
MAILING ADDRESS OF DEBTOR (If different from street address)	MAILING ADDRESS OF JOINT DEBTOR (If different from street address)

LOCATION OF PRINCIPAL ASSETS OF BUSINESS DEBTOR (If different from address listed above)	VENUE (Check one box) ☐ Debtor has been domiciled or has had a residence principal place of business, or principal assets in this District for 180 days immediately preceding the date of this petition or for a longer part of such 180 days than in any other District. ☐ There is a bankruptcy case concerning debtor's affiliate, general partner, or partnership pending in this District.

INFORMATION REGARDING DEBTOR (Check applicable boxes)

TYPE OF DEBTOR
☐ Individual
☐ Joint (Husband and Wife)
☐ Partnership
☐ Other _____   ☐ Corporation Publicly Held
   ☐ Corporation Not Publicly Held
   ☐ Municipality
	CHAPTER OR SECTION OF BANKRUPTCY CODE UNDER WHICH THE PETITION IS FILED (Check one box)
	☐ Chapter 7 ☐ Chapter 11 ☐ Chapter 13
	☐ Chapter 9 ☐ Chapter 12 ☐ Sec. 304 - Case Ancilary to Foreign Processing

NATURE OF DEBT ☐ Non-Business/Consumer ☐ Business - Complete A & B below **A. TYPE OF BUSINESS (Check one)** ☐ Farming ☐ Transportation ☐ Commodity Broker ☐ Professional ☐ Manufacturing/ ☐ Construction ☐ Retail/Wholesale Mining ☐ Real Estate ☐ Railroad ☐ Stockbroker ☐ Other Business **B. BRIEFLY DESCRIBE NATURE OF BUSINESS**	**FILING FEE (Check one box)** ☐ Filing fee attached ☐ Filing fee to be paid in installments. (Applicable to individuals only.) Must attach signed application for the court's consideration certifying that the debtor is unable to pay fee except in installments. Rule 1006(b). See Official Form No. 3 NAME AND ADDRESS OF LAW FIRM OR ATTORNEY Telephone No. NAME(S) OF ATTORNEY(S) DESIGNATED TO REPRESENT DEBTOR (Print or Type Names) ☐ Debtor is not represented by an attorney

STATISTICAL/ADMINISTRATIVE INFORMATION (U.S.C. § 604) (Estimates only) (Check applicable boxes)	THIS SPACE FOR COURT USE ONLY

☐ Debtor estimates that funds will be available for distribution to unsecured creditors.

☐ Debtor estimates that, after any exempt property is excluded and administrative expenses paid, there will be no funds available for distribution to unsecured creditors.

ESTIMATED NUMBER OF CREDITORS

1-15	16-49	50-99	100-199	200-999	1000-over
☐	☐	☐	☐	☐	☐

ESTIMATED ASSETS (In thousands of dollars)

Under 50	50-99	100-499	500-999	1000-9999	10,000-99,000	100,000-over
☐	☐	☐	☐	☐	☐	☐

ESTIMATED LIABILITIES (In thousands of dollars)

Under 50	50-99	100-499	500-999	1000-9999	10,000-99,000	100,000-over
☐	☐	☐	☐	☐	☐	☐

EST. NO. OF EMPLOYEES - CH. 11 & 12 ONLY

0	1-19	20-99	100-999	1000-over
☐	☐	☐	☐	☐

EST. NO. OF EQUITY SECURITY HOLDERS - CH. 11 & 12 ONLY

0	1-19	20-99	100-499	500-over
☐	☐	☐	☐	☐

PERSONAL BANKRUPTCY

Name of Debtor _____

Case No _____

FILING OF PLAN

For Chapter 9, 11, 12 and 13 cases only. Check appropriate box.

☐ A copy of debtor's proposed plan dated _____ is attached

☐ Debtor intends to file a plan within the time allowed by statute, rule or order of the court

PRIOR BANKRUPTCY CASE FILED WITHIN LAST 6 YEARS (If more than one, attach additional sheet)

Location Where Filed	Case Number	Date Filed

PENDING BANKRUPTCY CASE FILED BY ANY SPOUSE, PARTNER, OR AFFILIATE OF THE DEBTOR (If more than one, attach additional sheet)

Name of Debtor	Case Number	Date
Relationship	District	Judge

REQUEST FOR RELIEF

Debtor requests relief in accordance with the chapter of title 11, United States Code specified in this petition

SIGNATURES

ATTORNEY

X_____
Signature

Date _____

INDIVIDUAL JOINT DEBTOR(S)	CORPORATE OR PARTNERSHIP DEBTOR
I declare under penalty of perjury that the information provided in this petition is true and correct	I declare under penalty of perjury that the information provided in this petition is true and correct and that the filing of this petition on behalf of the debtor has been authorized
X_____ Signature of Debtor	X_____ Signature of Authorized Individual
Date _____	Print or Type Name of Authorized Individual
X_____ Signature of Joint Debtor	Title of Individual Authorized by Debtor to File this Petition
Date _____	Date _____

EXHIBIT "A" (To be completed if debtor is a corporation, requesting relief under Chapter 11.)

☐ Exhibit "A" is attached and made a part of this petition

TO BE COMPLETED BY INDIVIDUAL CHAPTER 7 DEBTOR WITH PRIMARILY CONSUMER DEBTS (See P.L. 98-353 § 322)

I am aware that I may proceed under chapter 7, 11, or 12, or 13 of title 11, United States Code, understand the relief available under such chapter, and choose to proceed under chapter 7 of such title

If I am represented by an attorney Exhibit B has been completed

X_____
Signature of Debtor

Date _____

X_____
Signature of Joint Debtor

Date _____

EXHIBIT "B" (To be completed by attorney for individual chapter 7 debtor(s) with primarily consumer debts.)

I, the attorney for the debtor(s) named in the foregoing petition, declare that I have informed the debtor(s) that (he, she, or they) may proceed under chapter 7, 11, 12, or 13 of title 11, United States Code, and have explained the relief available under such chapter.

X_____
Signature of Attorney

Date _____

Appendix A

Form B3
6/90

Form 3. APPLICATION AND ORDER TO PAY FILING FEE IN INSTALLMENTS

[Caption as in Form 16B.]

APPLICATION TO PAY FILING FEES IN INSTALLMENTS

In accordance with Fed. R. Bankr. P. 1006, application is made for permission to pay the filing fee on the following terms:

$ _____ with the filing of the petition, and the balance of

$ _____ in _____ installments, as follows:

    $ _____ on or before _____

    $ _____ on or before _____

    $ _____ on or before _____

    $ _____ on or before _____

I certify that I am unable to pay the filing fee except in installments. I further certify that I have not paid any money or transferred any property to an attorney or any other person for services in connection with this case or in connection with any other pending bankruptcy case and that I will not make any payment or transfer any property for services in connection with the case until the filing fee is paid in full.

Date: _____

_____
Applicant

_____
Address of Applicant

_____

ORDER

IT IS ORDERED that the debtor pay the filing fee in installments on the terms set forth in the foregoing application.

IT IS FURTHER ORDERED that until the filing fee is paid in full the debtor shall not pay, and no person shall accept, any money for services in connection with this case, and the debtor shall not relinquish, and no person shall accept, any property as payment for services in connection with this case.

BY THE COURT

Date: _____

_____
United States Bankruptcy Judge

139

PERSONAL BANKRUPTCY

FORM B5
(6/90)

FORM 5. INVOLUNTARY PETITION

United States Bankruptcy Court District of _____	INVOLUNTARY PETITION

IN RE (Name of debtor - If individual, enter: Last, First, Middle)	ALL OTHER NAMES used by debtor in the last 6 years (Include married, maiden, and trade names)
SOC SEC./TAX I.D. NO. (If more than one, state all)	
STREET ADDRESS OF DEBTOR (No. and street, city, state, and zip code)	MAILING ADDRESS OF DEBTOR (If different from street address)
COUNTY OR RESIDENCE OR PRINCIPAL PLACE OF BUSINESS	

LOCATION OF PRINCIPAL ASSETS OF BUSINESS DEBTOR (If different from previously listed addresses)

CHAPTER OF BANKRUPTCY CODE UNDER WHICH PETITION IS FILED

☐ Chapter 7   ☐ Chapter 11

INFORMATION REGARDING DEBTOR (Check applicable boxes)

Petitioners believe

☐ Debts are primarily consumer debts
☐ Debts are primarily business debts (Complete sections A and B)

TYPE OF DEBTOR

☐ Individual   ☐ Corporation Publicly Held
☐ Partnership   ☐ Corporation Not Publicly Held
☐ Other _____

A. TYPE OF BUSINESS (Check one)

☐ Professional   ☐ Transportation   ☐ Commodity Broker
☐ Retail/Wholesale   ☐ Manufacturing/   ☐ Construction
☐ Railroad   Mining   ☐ Real Estate
    ☐ Stockbroker   ☐ Other

B. BRIEFLY DESCRIBE NATURE OF BUSINESS

VENUE

☐ Debtor has been domiciled or has had a residence, principal place of business, or principal assets in the District for 180 days immediately preceding the date of this petition or for a longer part of such 180 days than in any other District.

☐ A bankruptcy case concerning debtor's affiliate, general partner or partnership is pending in this District.

PENDING BANKRUPTCY CASE FILED BY OR AGAINST ANY PARTNER OR AFFILIATE OF THIS DEBTOR (Report information for any additional cases on attached sheets.)

Name of Debtor	Case Number	Date
Relationship	District	Judge

ALLEGATIONS (Check applicable boxes)	COURT USE ONLY

1. ☐ Petitioner(s) are eligible to file this petition pursuant to 11 U.S.C. §303(b).
2. ☐ The debtor is a person against whom an order for relief may be entered under title 11 of the United States Code.

3.a. ☐ The debtor is generally not paying such debtor's debts as they become due, unless such debts are the subject of a bona fide dispute;

         or

  b. ☐ Within 120 days preceding the filing of this petition, a custodian, other than a trustee, receiver, or agent appointed or authorized to take charge of less than substantially all of the property of the debtor for the purpose of enforcing a lien against such property, was appointed or took possession.

140

Appendix A

FORM 5   Involuntary Petition
(10/89)

Name of Debtor _____

Case No. _____

(Court use only)

TRANSFER OF CLAIM

☐ Check this box if there has been a transfer of any claim against the debtor by or to any petitioner. Attach all documents evidencing the transfer and any statements that are required under Bankruptcy Rule 1003(a).

REQUEST FOR RELIEF

Petitioner(s) request that an order for relief be entered against the debtor under the chapter of title 11, United States Code, specified in this petition.

Petitioner(s) declare under penalty of perjury that the foregoing is true and correct according to the best of their knowledge, information, and belief.

X_____
Signature of Petitioner or Representative (State title)

X_____
Signature of Attorney

Name of Petitioner _____

Name of Attorney Firm (If any) _____

Name & Mailing
Address of Individual
Signing in Representative
Capacity

Address _____

Telephone No. _____

X_____
Signature of Petitioner or Representative (State title)

X_____
Signature of Attorney

Name of Petitioner _____

Name of Attorney Firm (If any) _____

Name & Mailing
Address of Individual
Signing in Representative
Capacity

Address _____

Telephone No. _____

X_____
Signature of Petitioner or Representative (State title)

X_____
Signature of Attorney

Name of Petitioner _____

Name of Attorney Firm (If any) _____

Name & Mailing
Address of Individual
Signing in Representative
Capacity

Address _____

Telephone No. _____

PETITIONING CREDITORS

Name and Address of Petitioner	Nature of Claim	Amount of Claim
Name and Address of Petitioner	Nature of Claim	Amount of Claim
Name and Address of Petitioner	Nature of Claim	Amount of Claim
Note: If there are more than three petitioners, attach additional sheets with the statement under penalty of perjury, petitioner(s) signatures under the statement and the name(s) of attorney(s) and petitioning creditor information in the format above.		Total Amount of Petitioners' Claims

____ continuation sheets attached

141

PERSONAL BANKRUPTCY

FORM B6A
(10/89)

In re _____ .   Case No._____
                    Debtor   (If known)

SCHEDULE A - REAL PROPERTY

Except as directed below, list all real property in which the debtor has any legal, equitable, or future interest, including all property owned as a co-tenant, community property, or in which the debtor has a life estate. Include any property in which the debtor holds rights and powers exercisable for the debtor's own benefit. If the debtor is married, state whether husband, wife, or both own the property by placing an "H," "W," "J," or "C" in the column labeled "Husband, Wife, Joint, or Community)." If the debtor holds no interest in real property, write "None" under "Description and Location of Property."

Do not include interests in executory contracts and unexpired leases on this schedule. List them in Schedule G - Executory Contracts and Unexpired Leases.

If an entity claims to have a lien or hold a secured interest in any property, state the amount of the secured claim. See Schedule D. If no entity claims to hold a secured interest in the property, write "None" in the column labeled "Amount of Secured Claim."

If the debtor is an individual or if a joint petition is filed, state the amount of any exemption claimed in the property only in Schedule C - Property Claimed as Exempt.

DESCRIPTION AND LOCATION OF PROPERTY	NATURE OF DEBTOR'S INTEREST IN PROPERTY	HUSBAND, WIFE, JOINT OR COMMUNITY	CURRENT MARKET VALUE OF DEBTOR'S INTEREST IN PROPERTY WITHOUT DEDUCTING ANY SECURED CLAIM OR EXEMPTION	AMOUNT OF SECURED CLAIM

Total ► | $

(Report also on Summary of Schedules.)

142

Appendix A

RM B6B
0/89)

In re _____ .   Case No. _____
                  Debtor   (If known)

SCHEDULE B - PERSONAL PROPERTY

Except as directed below, list all personal property of the debtor of whatever kind. If the debtor has no property in one or more of the categories, place an "X" in the appropriate position in the column labeled "None." If additional space is needed in any category, attach a separate sheet properly identified with the case name, case number, and the number of the category. If the debtor is married, state whether husband, wife, or both own the property by placing an "H," "W," "J," or "C" in the column labeled "Husband, Wife, Joint, or Community." If the debtor is an individual or a joint petition is filed, state the amount of any exemptions claimed only in Schedule C - Property Claimed as Exempt.

Do not list interests in executory contracts and unexpired leases on this schedule. List them in Schedule G - Executory Contracts and Unexpired Leases.

If the property is being held for the debtor by someone else, state that person's name and address under "Description and Location of Property."

TYPE OF PROPERTY	NONE	DESCRIPTION AND LOCATION OF PROPERTY	HUSBAND, WIFE, JOINT, COMMUNITY	CURRENT MARKET VALUE OF DEBTOR'S INTEREST IN PROPERTY, WITHOUT DEDUCTING ANY SECURED CLAIM OR EXEMPTION
1. Cash on hand.				
2. Checking, savings or other financial accounts, certificates of deposit, or shares in banks, savings and loan, thrift, building and loan, and homestead associations, or credit unions, brokerage houses, or cooperatives.				
3. Security deposits with public utilities, telephone companies, landlords, and others.				
4. Household goods and furnishings, including audio, video, and computer equipment.				
5. Books, pictures and other art objects, antiques, stamp, coin, record, tape, compact disc, and other collections or collectibles.				
6. Wearing apparel.				
7. Furs and jewelry.				
8. Firearms and sports, photographic, and other hobby equipment.				
9. Interests in insurance policies. Name insurance company of each policy and itemize surrender or refund value of each.				
10. Annuities. Itemize and name each issuer.				

143

PERSONAL BANKRUPTCY

FORM B6B - Cont.
(10/89)

In re _____ .   Case No. _____
            Debtor   (If known)

SCHEDULE B - PERSONAL PROPERTY
(Continuation Sheet)

TYPE OF PROPERTY	NONE	DESCRIPTION AND LOCATION OF PROPERTY	HUSBAND, WIFE, JOINT COMMUNITY	CURRENT MARKET VALUE OF DEBTOR'S INTEREST IN PROPERTY, WITHOUT DEDUCTING ANY SECURED CLAIM OR EXEMPTION
11. Interests in IRA, ERISA, Keogh, or other pension or profit sharing plans. Itemize.				
12. Stock and interests in incorporated and unincorporated businesses. Itemize.				
13. Interests in partnerships or joint ventures. Itemize.				
14. Government and corporate bonds and other negotiable and non-negotiable instruments.				
15. Accounts Receivable.				
16. Alimony, maintenance, support, and property settlements to which the debtor is or may be entitled. Give particulars.				
17. Other liquidated debts owing debtor include tax refunds. Give particulars.				
18. Equitable or future interests, life estates, and rights or powers exercisable for the benefit of the debtor other than those listed in Schedule of Real Property.				
19. Contingent and non-contingent interests in estate of a decedent, death benefit plan, life insurance policy, or trust.				
20. Other contingent and unliquidated claims of every nature, including tax refunds, counterclaims of the debtor, and rights to setoff claims. Give estimated value of each.				
21. Patents, coprights, and other intellectual property. Give particulars.				
22. Licenses, franchises, and other general intangibles. Give particulars.				

144

Appendix A

ORM B6B - Cont.
0/89)

In re _____ .   Case No. _____
                    Debtor   (If known)

SCHEDULE B - PERSONAL PROPERTY
(Continuation Sheet)

TYPE OF PROPERTY	NONE	DESCRIPTION AND LOCATION OF PROPERTY	HUSBAND, WIFE, JOINT COMMUNITY	CURRENT MARKET VALUE OF DEBTOR'S INTEREST IN PROPERTY, WITH-OUT DEDUCTING ANY SECURED CLAIM OR EXEMPTION
23. Automobiles, trucks, trailers, and other vehicles.				
24. Boats, motort, and accessories.				
25. Aircraft and accessories				
26. Office equipment, furnishings, and supplies.				
27. Mahinery, fixtures, equipment and supplies used in business.				
28. Inventory.				
29. Animals.				
30. Crops - growing or harvested. Give particulars.				
31. Framing equipment and implements.				
32. Farm supplies, chemicals, and feed.				
33. Other personal property of any kind not already listed. Itemize.				

_____ continuation sheets attached   Total ► $

(Include amounts from any continuation
sheets attached. Report total also on
Summary of Schedules.)

145

PERSONAL BANKRUPTCY

FORM B6C
(6/90)

In re _____.   Case No. _____
         Debtor   (If known)

SCHEDULE C - PROPERTY CLAIMED AS EXEMPT

Debtor elects the exemption to which debtor is entitled under

(Check one box)

☐ 11 U.S.C. § 522(b)(1) Exemptions provided in 11 U.S.C. § 522(d). Note: These exemptions are available only in certain states.

☐ 11 U.S.C. § 522(b)(2) Exemptions available under applicable nonbankruptcy federal laws, state or local law where the debtor's domicile has been located for the 180 days immediately preceding the filing of the petition, or for a longer portion of the 180-day period than in any other place, and the debtor's interest as a tenant by the entirety or joint tenant to the extent the interest is exempt from process under applicable nonbankruptcy law.

DESCRIPTION OF PROPERTY	SPECIFY LAW PROVIDING EACH EXEMPTION	VALUE OF CLAIMED EXEMPTION	CURRENT MARKET VALUE OF PROPERTY WITHOUT DEDUCTING EXEMPTIONS

146

Appendix A

FORM B6D
(6/90)

In re _____ ,   Case No. _____
                    Debtor   (If known)

SCHEDULE D - CREDITORS HOLDING SECURED CLAIMS

State the name, mailing address, including zip code, and account number, if any, of all entities holding claims secured by property of the debtor as of the date of filing of the petition. List creditors holding all types of secured interests such as judgment liens, garnishments, statutory liens, mortgages, deeds of trust, and other security interests. List creditors in alphabetical order to the extent practicable. If all secured creditors will not fit on this page, use the continuation sheet provided.

If any entity other than a spouse in a joint case may be jointly liable on a claim, place an "X" in the column labeled "Codebtor," include the entity on the appropriate schedule of creditors, and complete Schedule H - Codebtors. If a joint petition is filed, state whether husband, wife, both of them, or the marital community may be liable on each claim by placing an "H," "W," "J," or "C" in the column labeled"Husband, Wife, Joint, or Community."

If the claim is contingent, place an "X" in the column labeled "Contingent." If the claim is unliquidated, place an "X" in the column labeled "Unliquidated." If the claim is disputed, place an "X" in the column labeled "Disputed." (You may need to place an "X" in more than one of these three columns.)

Report the total of all claims listed on this schedule in the box labeled "Total" on the last sheet of the completed schedule. Report this total also on the Summary of Schedules.

☐ Check this box if debtor has no creditors holding secured claims to report on this Schedule D.

CREDITOR'S NAME AND MAILING ADDRESS INCLUDING ZIP CODE	CODEBTOR	HUSBAND, WIFE, JOINT OR COMMUNITY	DATE CLAIM WAS INCURRED, NATURE OF LIEN, AND DESCRIPTION AND MARKET VALUE OF PROPERTY SUBJECT TO LIEN	CONTINGENT	UNLIQUIDATED	DISPUTED	AMOUNT OF CLAIM WITHOUT DEDUCTING VALUE OF COLLATERAL	UNSECURED PORTION, IF ANY
ACCOUNT NO.								
			Value $					
ACCOUNT NO.								
			Value $					
ACCOUNT NO.								
			Value $					
ACCOUNT NO.								
			Value $					

_____ Continuation sheets attached

Subtotal ➔ $
(Total of this page)
Total ➔ $
(Use only on last page)

(Report total also on Summary of Schedules)

147

PERSONAL BANKRUPTCY

FORM B6D - Cont.
(10/89)

In re _____ ,　　　Case No. _____
　　　　　　　　　　　　Debtor　　　　　　　　　　　　　　　　　　　　　　(If known)

SCHEDULE D - CREDITORS HOLDING SECURED CLAIMS
(Continuation Sheet)

CREDITOR'S NAME AND MAILING ADDRESS INCLUDING ZIP CODE	CODEBTOR HUSBAND, WIFE, JOINT OR COMMUNITY	DATE CLAIM WAS INCURRED, NATURE OF LIEN, AND DESCRIPTION AND MARKET VALUE OF PROPERTY SUBJECT TO LIEN	CONTINGENT	UNLIQUIDATED	DISPUTED	AMOUNT OF CLAIM WITHOUT DEDUCTING VALUE OF COLLATERAL	UNSECURED PORTION, IF ANY
ACCOUNT NO.							
		VALUE $					
ACCOUNT NO.							
		VALUE $					
ACCOUNT NO.							
		VALUE $					
ACCOUNT NO.							
		VALUE $					
ACCOUNT NO.							
		VALUE $					

Sheet _____ of _____ continuation sheets attached to Schedule of Creditors Holding Unsecured Claims　　Subtotal ► $ _____

(Total of this page)

Total ► $ _____

(Use only on last page)

(Report total also on Summary of Schedules)

148

Appendix A

FORM B6E
(6/90)

In re _____ .   Case No. _____
                        Debtor   (If known)

SCHEDULE E - CREDITORS HOLDING UNSECURED PRIORITY CLAIMS

A complete list of claims entitled to property, listed separately by type of priority, is to be set forth on the sheets provided. Only holders of unsecured claims entitled to priority should be listed in this schedule. In the boxes provided on the attached sheets, state the name and mailing address, including zip code, and account number if any, of all entities holding priority claims against the debtor or the property of the debtor, as of the date of the filing of this petition.

If any entity other than a spouse in a joint case may be jointly liable on a claim, place an "X" in the column labeled "Codebtor," include the entity on the appropriate schedule of creditors, and complete Schedule H - Codebtors. If a joint petition is filed, state whether husband, wife, both of them, or the marital community may be liable on each claim by placing an "H," "W," "J," or "C" in the column labeled "Husband, Wife, Joint, or Community."

If the claim is contingent, place an "X" in the column labeled "Contingent." If the claim is unliquidated, place an "X" in the column labeled "Unliquidated." If the claim is disputed, place an "X" in the column labeled "Disputed." (You may need to place an "X" in more than one of these three columns.)

Report the total of claims listed on each sheet in the box labeled, "Subtotal" on each sheet. Report the total of all claims listed on this Schedule E in the box labeled "Total" on the last sheet of the completed schedule. Repeat this total also on the Summary of Schedules.

☐ Check this box if debtor has no creditors holding unsecured priority claims to report on this Schedule E.

TYPES OF PRIORITY

☐ **Extensions of credit in an involuntary case**

Claims arising in the ordinary course of the debtor's business or financial affairs after the commencement of the case but before the earlier of the appointment of a trustee or the order for relief. 11 U.S.C. § 507(a)(2).

☐ **Wages, salaries, and commissions**

Wages, salaries, and commissions, including vacation, severance, and sick leave pay owing to employees, up to a maximum of $2000 per employee, earned within 90 days immediately preceding the filing of the original petition, or the cessation of business, whichever occurred first, to the extent provided in 11 U.S.C. § 507(a)(3).

☐ **Contributions to employee benefit plans**

Money owed to employee benefit plans for services rendered within 180 days immediately preceding the filing of the original petition, or the cessation of business, whichever occurred first, to the extent provided in 11 U.S.C. § 507(a)(4).

☐ **Certain farmers and fishermen**

Claims of certain farmers and fishermen, up to a maximum of $2000 per farmer or fisherman, against the debtor, as provided in 11 U.S.C. § 507(a)(5).

☐ **Deposits by individuals**

Claims of individuals up to a maximum of $900 for deposits for the purchase, lease, or rental of property or services for personal, family, or household use, that were not delivered or provided. 11 U.S.C. § 507(a)(6).

☐ **Taxes and Other Certain Debts Owed to Governmental**

Taxes, customs duties, and penalties owing to federal, state, and local governmental units as set forth in 11 U.S.C. §507(a)(7).

_____ continuation sheets attached

149

Personal Bankruptcy

FORM B6E - Cont.
(10/89)

In re _____.   Case No. _____
                    Debtor   (If known)

SCHEDULE E - CREDITORS, HOLDING UNSECURED PRIORITY CLAIMS
(Continuation Sheet)

TYPE OF PRIORITY

CREDITOR'S NAME AND MAILING ADDRESS INCLUDING ZIP CODE	CODEBTOR	HUSBAND, WIFE, JOINT OR COMMUNITY	DATE CLAIM WAS INCURRED AND CONSIDERATION FOR CLAIM	CONTINGENT	UNLIQUIDATED	DISPUTED	TOTAL AMOUNT OF CLAIM	AMOUNT ENTITLED TO PRIORITY
ACCOUNT NO.								
ACCOUNT NO.								
ACCOUNT NO.								
ACCOUNT NO.								
ACCOUNT NO.								

Sheet no. _____ of _____ sheets attached to Schedule of Creditors

Subtotal ▶ | $
(Total of this page)
Total ▶ | $
(Use only on last page of the completed Schedule E)

(Report total also on Summary of Schedules)

150

Appendix A

Form B6F
(10/89)

In re _____ .　　Case No. _____
　　　　　　Debtor　　　　　　　　　　　　　　　　　　　　　　　(If Known)

SCHEDULE F - CREDITORS HOLDING UNSECURED NONPRIORITY CLAIMS

State the name, mailing address, including zip code, and account number, if any, of all entities holding unsecured claims without priority against the debtor or the property of the debtor, as of the date of filing of the petition. Do not include claims listed in Schedules D and E. If all creditors will not fit on this page, use the continuation sheet provided.

If any entity other than a spouse in a joint case may be jointly liable on a claim, place an "X" in the column labeled "Codebtor," include the entity on the appropriate schedule of creditors, and complete Schedule H - Codebtors. If a joint petition is filed, state whether husband, wife, both of them, or the marital community may be liable on each claim by placing an "H," "W," "J," or "C" in the column labeled "Husband, Wife, Joint, or Community."

If the claim is contingent, place an "X" in the column labeled "Contingent." If the claim is unliquidated, place an "X" in the column labeled "Unliquidated." If the claim is disputed, place an "X" in the column labeled "Disputed." (You may need to place an "X" in more than one of these three columns.)

Report total of all claims listed on this schedule in the box labeled "Total" on the last sheet of the completed schedule. Report this total also on the Summary of Schedules.

☐ Check this box if debtor has no creditors holding unsecured non priority claims to report on this Schedule F.

CREDITOR'S NAME AND MAILING ADDRESS INCLUDING ZIP CODE	CODEBTOR	HUSBAND, WIFE OR JOINT	DATE CLAIM WAS INCURRED AND CONSIDERATION FOR CLAIM, IF CLAIM IS SUBJECT TO SETOFF, SO STATE	CONTINGENT	UNLIQUIDATED	DISPUTED	AMOUNT OF CLAIM
ACCOUNT NO.							
ACCOUNT NO.							
ACCOUNT NO.							
ACCOUNT NO.							

_____ continuation sheets attached

Subtotal ➡ | $

Total ➡ | $

(Report total also on Summary of Schedules)

151

PERSONAL BANKRUPTCY

Form B6F
(10/89)

In re _____ ,   Case No. _____
                   Debtor   (If known)

SCHEDULE F - CREDITORS HOLDING UNSECURED NONPRIORITY
(Continuation Sheet)

CREDITOR'S NAME AND MAILING ADDRESS INCLUDING ZIP CODE	CODEBTOR	HUSBAND, WIFE OR JOINT	DATE CLAIM WAS INCURRED AND CONSIDERATION FOR CLAIM. IF CLAIM IS SUBJECT TO SETOFF, SO STATE	CONTINGENT	UNLIQUIDATED	DDISPUTED	AMOUNT OF CLAIM
ACCOUNT NO.							
ACCOUNT NO.							
ACCOUNT NO.							
ACCOUNT NO.							
ACCOUNT NO.							

Sheet no. _____ of _____ sheets attached to Schedule of
Creditors Holding Unsecured Nonpriority Claims

Subtotal ➤ $ _____
(Total of this page)
Total ➤ $ _____
(Use only on last page of the completed Schedule E)

(Report total also on Summary of Schedules)

Appendix A

Form B6G
(10/89)

In re _____.   Case No. _____
                        Debtor   (If Known)

SCHEDULE G - EXECUTORY CONTRACTS AND UNEXPIRED LEASES

Describe all executory contracts of any nature and all unexpired leases of real or personal property. Include any timeshare interests.

State nature of debtor's interest in contract, i.e., "Purchaser," "Agent," etc. State whether debtor is the lessor or lessee of a lease.

Provide the names and complete mailing addresses of all other parties to each lease or contract described.

NOTE: A party listed on this schedule will not receive notice of the filing of this case unless the party is also scheduled in the appropriate schedule of creditors.

☐ Check this box if debtor has no executory contracts or unexpired leases.

NAME AND MAILING ADDRESS, INCLUDING ZIP CODE, OF OTHER PARTIES TO LEASE OR CONTRACT	DESCRIPTION OF CONTRACT OR LEASE AND NATURE OF DEBTOR'S INTEREST, STATE WHETHER LEASE IS FOR NONRESIDENTIAL REAL PROPERTY. STATE CONTRACT NUMBER OF ANY GOVERNMENT CONTRACT

PERSONAL BANKRUPTCY

Form B6H
(6/90)

In re _____ .   Case No. _____
          Debtor   (If known)

SCHEDULE H - CODEBTORS

Provide the information requested concerning any person or entity, other than a spouse in a joint case, that is also liable on any debts listed by debtor in the schedules of creditors. Include all guarantors and co-signers. In community property states, a married debtor not filing a joint case should report the name and address of the nondebtor spouse on this schedule. Include all names used by the nondebtor spouse during the six years immediately preceding the commencement of this case.

☐ Check this box if debtor has no codebtors.

NAME AND ADDRESS OF CODEBTOR	NAME AND ADDRESS OF CREDITOR

154

Appendix A

Form B6I
(6/90)

In re _____ .   Case No. _____
                    Debtor   (If known)

SCHEDULE I - CURRENT INCOME OF INDIVIDUAL DEBTOR(S)

The column labeled "Spouse" must be completed in all cases filed by joint debtors and by a married debtor in a chapter 12 or 13 case whether or not a joint petition is filed, unless the spouses are separated and a joint petition is not filed.

Debtor's Marital Status:	DEPENDENTS OF DEBTOR AND SPOUSE		
	NAMES	AGE	RELATIONSHIP

EMPLOYMENT :	DEBTOR	SPOUSE
Occupation Name of Employer		
How long employed		
Address of Employer		

	DEBTOR	SPOUSE
Income: (Estimate of average monthly income)		
Current monthly gross wages, salary, and commissions (pro rate if not paid monthly.)	$ _____	$ _____
Estimated monthly overtime	$ _____	$ _____
SUBTOTAL	$ _____	$ _____
LESS PAYROLL DEDUCTIONS		
a. Payroll taxes and social security	$ _____	$ _____
b. Insurance	$ _____	$ _____
c. Union dues	$ _____	$ _____
d. Other (Specify _____)	$ _____	$ _____
SUBTOTAL OF PAYROLL DEDUCTIONS	$ _____	$ _____
TOTAL NET MONTHLY TAKE HOME PAY	$ _____	$ _____
Regular income from operation of business or profession or farm (attach detailed statement)	$ _____	$ _____
Income from real property	$ _____	$ _____
Interest and dividends	$ _____	$ _____
Alimony, maintenance or support payments payable to the debtor for the debtor's use or that of dependents listed above.	$ _____	$ _____
Social security or other government assistance (Specify) _____	$ _____	$ _____
Pension or retirement income	$ _____	$ _____
Other monthly income	$ _____	$ _____
(Specify) _____	$ _____	$ _____
	$ _____	$ _____
TOTAL MONTHLY INCOME	$ _____	$ _____

TOTAL COMBINED MONTHLY INCOME $_____   (Report also on Summary of Schedules)

Describe any increase or decrease of more than 10% in any of the above categories anticipated to occur within the year following the filing of this document:

155

PERSONAL BANKRUPTCY

FORM B6J
(6/90)

In re _____ ,   Case No. _____
              Debtor   (If known)

SCHEDULE J - CURRENT EXPENDITURES OF INDIVIDUAL DEBTORS

Complete this schedule by estimating the average monthly expenses of the debtor and the debtor's family. Pro rate any payments made bi-weekly, quarterly, semi-annually, or annually to show monthly rate.

☐ Check this box if a joint petition is filed and debtor's spouse maintains a separate household. Complete a separate schedule of expenditures labeled "Spouse."

Rent or home mortgage payment (include lot rented for mobile home)	$ _____
Are real estate taxes included? Yes _____ No _____	
Is property insurance included? Yes _____ No _____	
Utilities Electricity and heating fuel	$ _____
Water and sewer	$ _____
Telephone	$ _____
Other _____	$ _____
Home Maintenance (Repairs and upkeep)	$ _____
Food	$ _____
Clothing	$ _____
Laundry and dry cleaning	$ _____
Medical and dental expenses	$ _____
Transportation (not including car payments)	$ _____
Recreation, clubs and entertainment, newspapers, magazines, etc.	$ _____
Charitable contributions	$ _____
Insurance (not deducted from wages or included in home mortgage payments)	
Homeowner's or renter's	$ _____
Life	$ _____
Health	$ _____
Auto	$ _____
Other _____	$ _____
Taxes (not deducted from wages or included in home mortgage payuments)	
(Specify) _____	$ _____
Installment payments (In chapter 12 and 13 cases, do not list payments to be included in the plan)	
Auto	$ _____
Other _____	$ _____
Other _____	$ _____
Alimony, maintenance, and support paid to others	$ _____
Payments for support of additional dependents not living at your home	$ _____
Regular expenses from operation of business, profession, or farm (attach detailed statement)	$ _____
Other _____	$ _____

TOTAL MONTHLY EXPENSES (Report also on Summary of Schedules) $ _____

(FOR CHAPTER 12 DEBTORS ONLY)
Provide the information requested below, including whether plan payments are to be made bi-weekly, monthly, annually, or at some other regular interval.

A. Total projected monthly income	$ _____
B. Total projected monthly expenses	$ _____
C. Excess income (A minus B)	$ _____
D. Total amount to be paid into plan each _____	$ _____
(interval)	

Appendix A

FORM B6 - Cont.
(6/90)

In re _____ ,   Case No. _____
                        Debtor   (If known)

DECLARATION CONCERNING DEBTOR'S SCHEDULES

DECLARATION UNDER PENALTY OF PERJURY BY INDIVIDUAL DEBTOR

I declare under penalty of perjury that I have read the foregoing summary and schedules, consisting of _____ sheets,
and that they are true and correct to the best of my knowledge, information, and belief.   (Total shown on summary page plus 1)

Date _____   Signature _____
                                                                        Debtor

Date _____   Signature _____
                                                                (Joint Debtor, if any)
                                                          [If joint case, both spouses must sign.]

- -

DECLARATION UNDER PENALTY OF PERJURY ON BEHALF OF CORPORATION OR PARTNERSHIP

I, the _____ [the president or other officer or an authorized agent of the corporation or a member or an
authorized agent of the partnership] of the _____ [corporation or partnership] named as debtor in this case,
declare under penalty of perjury that I have read the following summary and schedules, consisting of _____ sheets, and that
they are true and correct to the best of my knowledge, information, and belief.   (Total shown on summary page plus 1)

Date _____

                                              Signature _____

                                                          _____
                                                          [Print or type name of individual signing on behalf of debtor]

[An individual signing on behalf of a partnership or corporation must indicate position or relationship to debtor.]

- -

Penalty for making a false statement or concealing property. Fine of up to $500,000 or imprisonment for up to 5 years or both. 18 U.S.C. §§ 152 and 3571.

157

FORM B6 - Cont.
(6/90)

United States Bankruptcy Court

_____ District of _____

In re _____,   Case No. _____
                    Debtor   (If known)

SUMMARY OF SCHEDULES

Indicate as to each schedule whether that schedule is attached and state the number of pages in each. Report the totals from Schedules A, B, D, E, F, I, and J in the boxes provided. Add the amounts from Schedules A and B to determine the total amount of the debtor's assets. Add the amounts from Schedules D, E, and F to determine the total amount of the debtor's liabilities.

NAME OF SCHEDULE	ATTACHED (YES/NO)	NO. OF SHEETS	AMOUNTS SCHEDULED		
			ASSETS	LIABILITIES	OTHER
A - Real Property		$			
B - Personal Property		$			
C - Property Claimed As Exempt					
D - Creditor Holding Secured Claims				$	
E - Creditors Holding Unsecured Priority Claims				$	
F - Creditors Holding Unsecured Nonproperty Claims				$	
G - Executory Contracts and Unexpired Leases					
H - Codebtors					
I - Current Income of Individual Debtor(s)					$
J - Current Expenditures of Individual Debtor(s)					$
Total Number of sheets in ALL Schedules ►					
Total Assets ►			$		
Total Liabilities ►				$	

158

Appendix A

Form B6
(6/90)

FORM 6. SCHEDULES

Summary of Schedules

Schedule A - Real Property

Schedule B - Personal Property

Schedule C - Property Claimed as Exempt

Schedule D - Creditors Holding Secured Claims

Schedule E - Creditors Holding Unsecured Priority Claims

Schedule F - Creditors Holding Unsecured Nonpriority Claims

Schedule G - Executory Contracts and Unexpired Leases

Schedule H - Codebtors

Schedule I - Current Income of Individual Debtor(s)

Schedule J - Current Expenditures of Individual Debtor(s)

Unsworn Declaration under Penalty of Perjury

GENERAL INSTRUCTIONS: The first page of the debtor's schedules and the first page of any amendments thereto must contain a caption as in Form 16B. Subsequent pages should be identified with the debtor's name and case number. If the schedules are filed with the petition, the case number should be left blank.

Schedules D, E, and F have been designed for the listing of each claim only once. Even when a claim is secured only in part or entitled to priority only in part, it still should be listed only once. A claim which is secured in whole or in part should be listed on Schedule D only, and a claim which is entitled to priority in whole or in part should be listed on Schedule E only. Do not list the same claim twice. If a creditor has more than one claim, such as claims arising from separate transactions, each claim should be scheduled separately.

Review the specific instructions for each schedule before completing the schedule.

PERSONAL BANKRUPTCY

FORM 7
(6/90)

FORM 7. STATEMENT OF FINANCIAL AFFAIRS

UNITED STATES BANKRUPTCY COURT
_____ District of _____

In Re: _____ .   Case No._____
                    (Name)   (If Known)
                              Debtor

STATEMENT OF FINANCIAL AFFAIRS

     This statement is to be completed by every debtor. Spouses filing a joint petition may file a single statement on which the information for both spouses is combined. If the case is filed under chapter 12 or chapter 13, a married debtor must furnish information for both spouses whether or not a joint petition is filed, unless the spouses are separated and a joint petition is not filed. An individual debtor engaged in business as a sole proprietor, partner, family farmer, or self-employed professional, should provide the information requested on this statement concerning all such activities as well as the individual's personal affairs.

     Questions 1 - 15 are to be completed by all debtors. Debtors that are or have been in business, as defined below, also must complete Questions 16 - 21. **Each question must be answered. If the answer to any question is "None," or the question is not applicable, mark the box labeled "None."** If additional space is needed for the answer to any question, use and attach a separate sheet properly identified with the case name, case number (if known), and the number of the question.

DEFINITIONS

     "In business." A debtor is "in business" for the purpose of this form if the debtor is a corporation or partnership. An individual debtor is "in business" for the purpose of this form if the debtor is or has been, within the two years immediately preceding the filing of the this bankruptcy case, any of the following: an officer, director, managing executive, or person in control of a corporation; a partner, other than a limited partner, of a partnership; a sole proprietor or self-employed.

     "Insider." The term "insider" includes but is not limited to: relatives of the debtor; general partners of the debtor and their relatives; corporations of which the debtor is an officer, director, or person in control; officers, directors, and any person in control of a corporate debtor and their relatives; affiliates of the debtor and insiders of such affiliates; any managing agent of the debtor. 11 U.S.C. § 101(30).

---

1. Income from employment or operation of business

None
☐
     State the gross amount of income the debtor has received from employment, trade, or profession, or from operation of the debtor's business from the beginning of this calendar year to the date this case was commenced. State also the gross amounts received during the **two years** immediately preceding this calendar year. (A debtor that maintains, or has maintained, financial records on the basis of a fiscal rather than a calendar year may report fiscal year income. Identify the beginning and ending dates of the debtor's fiscal year.) If a joint petition is filed, state income for each spouse separately. (Married debtors filing under chapter 12 or chapter 13 must state income of both spouses whether or not a joint petition is filed, unless the spouses are separated and a joint petition is not filed.)

AMOUNT   SOURCE (if more than one)

Appendix A

2. Income other than from employment or operation of business

None ☐ State the amount of income received by the debtor other than from employment, trade, profession, or operation of the debtor's business during the **two years** immediately preceding the commencement of this case. Give particulars. If a joint petition is filed, state income for each spouse separately. (Married debtors filing under chapter 12 or chapter 13 must state income for each spouse whether or not a joint petition is filed, unless the spouses are separated and a joint petition is not filed.)

AMOUNT   SOURCE

---

3. Payments to creditors

None ☐ a. List all payments on loans, installment purchases of goods or services, and other debts, aggregating more than $600 to any creditor, made within **90 days** immediately preceding the commencement of this case. (Married debtors filing under chapter 12 or chapter 13 must include payments by either or both spouses whether or not a joint petition is filed, unless the spouses are separated and a joint petition is not filed.)

NAME AND ADDRESS OF CREDITOR	DATES OF PAYMENTS	AMOUNT PAID	AMOUNT STILL OWING

None ☐ b. List all payments made within **one year** immediately preceding the commencement of this case to or for the benefit of creditors who are or were insiders. (Married debtors filing under chapter 12 or chapter 13 must include payments by either or both spouses whether or not a joint petition is filed, unless the spouses are separated and a joint petition is not filed.)

NAME AND ADDRESS OF CREDITOR AND RELATIONSHIP TO DEBTOR	DATE OF PAYMENT	AMOUNT PAID	AMOUNT STILL OWING

---

4. Suits, executions, garnishments and attachments

None ☐ a. List all suits to which the debtor is or was a party within **one year** immediately preceding the filing of this bankruptcy case. (Married debtors filing under chapter 12 or chapter 13 must include information concerning either or both spouses whether or not a joint petition is filed, unless the spouses are separated and a joint petition is not filed.)

CAPTION OF SUIT AND CASE NUMBER	NATURE OF PROCEEDING	COURT AND LOCATION	STATUS OR DISPOSITION

Personal Bankruptcy

None b. Describe all property that has been attached, garnished or seized under any legal or equitable
☐ process within **one year** immediately preceding the commencement of this case. (Married debtors filing under chapter 12 or chapter 13 must include information concerning property of either or both spouses whether or not a joint petition is filed, unless the spouses are separated and a joint petition is not filed.)

NAME AND ADDRESS OF PERSON FOR WHOSE BENEFIT PROPERTY WAS SEIZED	DATE OF SEIZURE	DESCRIPTION AND VALUE OF PROPERTY

---

5. Repossessions, foreclosures and returns

None List all property that has been repossessed by a creditor, sold at a foreclosure sale, transferred
☐ through a deed in lieu of foreclosure or returned to the seller, within **one year** immediately preceding the commencement of this case. (Married debtors filing under chapter 12 or chapter 13 must include information concerning property of either or both spouses whether or not a joint petition is filed, unless the spouses are separated and a joint petition is not filed.)

NAME AND ADDRESS OF CREDITOR OR SELLER	DATE OF REPOSSESSION, FORECLOSURE SALE, TRANSFER OR RETURN	DESCRIPTION AND VALUE OF PROPERTY

---

6. Assignments and receiverships

None a. Describe any assignment of property for the benefit of creditors made within **120 days** immediately
☐ preceding the commencement of this case. (Married debtors filing under chapter 12 or chapter 13 must include any assignment by either or both spouses whether or not a joint petition is filed, unless the spouses are separated and a joint petition is not filed.)

NAME AND ADDRESS OF ASSIGNEE	DATE OF ASSIGNMENT	TERMS OF ASSIGNMENT OR SETTLEMENT

None b. List all property which has been in the hands of a custodian, receiver, or court-appointed official
☐ within **one year** immediately preceding the commencement of this case. (Married debtors filing under chapter 12 or chapter 13 must include information concerning property of either or both spouses whether or not a joint petition is filed, unless the spouses are separated and a joint petition is not filed.)

NAME AND ADDRESS OF CUSTODIAN	NAME AND LOCATION OF COURT CASE TITLE & NUMBER	DATE OF ORDER	DESCRIPTION AND VALUE OF PROPERTY

Appendix A

7. Gifts

None

☐

List all gifts or charitable contributions made within **one year** immediately preceding the commencement of this case except ordinary and usual gifts to family members aggregating less than $200 in value per individual family member and charitable contributions aggregating less than $100 per recipient. (Married debtors filing under chapter 12 or chapter 13 must include gifts or contributions by either or both spouses whether or not a joint petition is filed, unless the spouses are separated and a joint petition is not filed.)

NAME AND ADDRESS OF PERSON OR ORGANIZATION	RELATIONSHIP TO DEBTOR, IF ANY	DATE OF GIFT	DESCRIPTION AND VALUE OF GIFT

8. Losses

None

☐

List all losses from fire, theft, other casualty or gambling within **one year** immediately preceding the commencement of this case **or since the commencement of this case.** (Married debtors filing under chapter 12 or chapter 13 must include losses by either or both spouses whether or not a joint petition is filed, unless the spouses are separated and a joint petition is not filed.)

DESCRIPTION AND VALUE OF PROPERTY	DESCRIPTION OF CIRCUMSTANCES AND, IF LOSS WAS COVERED IN WHOLE OR IN PART BY INSURANCE, GIVE PARTICULARS	DATE OF LOSS

9. Payments related to debt counseling or bankruptcy

None

☐

List all payments made or property transferred by or on behalf of the debtor to any persons, including attorneys, for consultation concerning debt consolidation, relief under the bankruptcy law or preparation of a petition in bankruptcy within **one year** immediately preceding the commencement of this case.

NAME AND ADDRESS OF PAYEE	DATE OF PAYMENT, NAME OF PAYOR IF OTHER THAN DEBTOR	AMOUNT OF MONEY OR DESCRIPTION AND VALUE OF PROPERTY

10. Other transfers

None ☐ a. List all other property, other than property transferred in the ordinary course of the business or financial affairs of the debtor, transferred either absolutely or as security within **one year** immediately preceding the commencement of this case. (Married debtors filing under chapter 12 or chapter 13 must include transfers by either or both spouses whether or not a joint petition is filed, unless the spouses are separated and a joint petition is not filed.)

NAME AND ADDRESS OF TRANSFEREE, RELATIONSHIP TO DEBTOR	DATE	DESCRIBE PROPERTY TRANSFERRED AND VALUE RECEIVED

11. Closed financial accounts

None ☐ List all financial accounts and instruments held in the name of the debtor or for the benefit of the debtor which were closed, sold, or otherwise transferred within **one year** immediately preceding the commencement of this case. Include checking, savings, or other financial accounts, certificates of deposit, or other instruments; shares and share accounts held in banks, credit unions, pension funds, cooperatives, associations, brokerage houses and other financial institutions. (Married debtors filing under chapter 12 or chapter 13 must include information concerning accounts or instruments held by or for either or both spouses whether or not a joint petition is filed, unless the spouses are separated and a joint petition is not filed.)

NAME AND ADDRESS OF INSTITUTION	TYPE AND NUMBER OF ACCOUNT AND AMOUNT OF FINAL BALANCE	AMOUNT AND DATE OF SALE OR CLOSING

12. Safe deposit boxes

None ☐ List each safe deposit or other box or depository in which the debtor has or had securities, cash, or other valuables within **one year** immediately preceding the commencement of this case. (Married debtors filing under chapter 12 or chapter 13 must include boxes or depositories of either or both spouses whether or not a joint petition is filed, unless the spouses are separated and a joint petition is not filed.)

NAME AND ADDRESS OF BANK OR OTHER DEPOSITORY	NAMES AND ADDRESSES OF THOSE WITH ACCESS TO BOX OR DEPOSITORY	DESCRIPTION OF CONTENTS	DATE OF TRANSFER OR SURRENDER, IF ANY

Appendix A

13. Setoffs

None
☐
List all setoffs made by any creditor, including a bank, against a debt or deposit of the debtor within **90 days** preceding the commencement of this case. (Married debtors filing under chapter 12 or chapter 13 must include information concerning either or both spouses whether or not a joint petition is filed, unless the spouses are separated and a joint petition is not filed.)

NAME AND ADDRESS OF CREDITOR	DATE OF SETOFF	AMOUNT OF SETOFF

14. Property held for another person

None
☐
List all property owned by another person that the debtor holds or controls.

NAME AND ADDRESS OF OWNER	DESCRIPTION AND VALUE OF PROPERTY	LOCATION OF PROPERTY

15. Prior address of debtor

None
☐
If the debtor has moved within the **two years** immediately preceding the commencement of this case, list all premises which the debtor occupied during that period and vacated prior to the commencement of this case. If a joint petition is filed, report also any separate address of either spouse.

ADDRESS	NAME USED	DATES OF OCCUPANCY

165

Personal Bankruptcy

The following questions are to be completed by every debtor that is a corporation or partnership and by any individual debtor who is or has been, within the two years immediately preceding the commencement of this case, any of the following: an officer, director, managing executive, or owner of more than 5 percent of the voting securities of a corporation; a partner, other than a limited partner, of a partnership; a sole proprietor or otherwise self-employed.

(An individual or joint debtor should complete this portion of the statement only if the debtor is or has been in business, as defined above, within the two years immediately preceding the commencement of this case.)

16. Nature, location and name of business

None ☐ a. If the debtor is an individual, list the names and addresses of all businesses in which the debtor was an officer, director, partner, or managing executive of a corporation, partnership, sole proprietorship, or was a self-employed professional within the two years immediately preceding the commencement of this case, or in which the debtor owned 5 percent or more of the voting or equity securities within the two years immediately preceding the commencement of this case.

b. If the debtor is a partnership, list the names and addresses of all businesses in which the debtor was a partner or owned 5 percent or more of the voting securities, within the **two years** immediately preceding the commencement of this case.

c. If the debtor is a corporation, list the names and addresses of all businesses in which the debtor was a partner or owned 5 percent or more of the voting securities within the **two years** immediately preceding the commencement of this case.

NAME	ADDRESS	NATURE OF BUSINESS	BEGINNING AND ENDING DATES OF OPERATION

17. Books, records and financial statements

None ☐ a. List all bookkeepers and accountants who within the **six years** immediately preceding the filing of this bankruptcy case kept or supervised the keeping of books of account and records of the debtor.

NAME AND ADDRESS	DATES SERVICES RENDERED

None ☐ b. List all firms or individuals who within the **two years** immediately preceding the filing of this bankruptcy case have audited the books of account and records, or prepared a financial statement of the debtor.

NAME	ADDRESS	DATES SERVICES RENDERED

166

Appendix A

None
☐
c. List all firms or individuals who at the time of the commencement of this case were in possession of the books of account and records of the debtor. If any of the books of account and records are not available, explain.

    NAME   ADDRESS

_____

None
☐
d. List all financial institutions, creditors and other parties, including mercantile and trade agencies, to whom a financial statement was issued within the **two years** immediately preceding the commencement of this case by the debtor.

    NAME AND ADDRESS   DATE ISSUED

_____

18. Inventories

None
☐
a. List the dates of the last two inventories taken of your property, the name of the person who supervised the taking of each inventory, and the dollar amount and basis of each inventory.

                                         DOLLAR AMOUNT OF INVENTORY
    DATE OF INVENTORY   INVENTORY   SUPERVISOR   (Specify cost, market or other basis)

_____

None
☐
b. List the name and address of the person having possession of the records of each of the two inventories reported in a., above.

                                  NAME AND ADDRESSES OF CUSTODIAN
    DATE OF INVENTORY   OF INVENTORY RECORDS

_____

19. Current Partners, Officers, Directors and Shareholders

None
☐
a. If the debtor is a partnership, list the nature and percentage of partnership interest of each member of the partnership.

    NAME AND ADDRESS   NATURE OF INTEREST   PERCENTAGE OF INTEREST

PERSONAL BANKRUPTCY

None
□
b. If the debtor is a corporation, list all officers and directors of the corporation, and each stockholder who directly or indirectly owns, controls, or holds 5 percent or more of the voting securities of the corporation.

NAME AND ADDRESS	TITLE	NATURE AND PERCENTAGE OF STOCK OWNERSHIP

---

20. Former partners, officers, directors and shareholders

None
□
a. If the debtor is a partnership, list each member who withdrew from the partnership within **one year** year immediately preceding the commencement of this case.

NAME	ADDRESS	DATE OF WITHDRAWAL

None
□
b. If the debtor is a corporation, list all officers, or directors whose relationship with the corporation terminated within **one year** immediately preceding the commencement of this case.

NAME AND ADDRESS	TITLE	DATE OF TERMINATION

---

21. Withdrawals from a partnership or distributions by a corporation

None
□
If the debtor is a partnership or corporation, list all withdrawals or distributions credited or given to an insider, including compensation in any form, bonuses, loans, stock redemptions, options exercised and any other perquisite during **one year** immediately preceding the commencement of this case.

NAME & ADDRESS OF RECIPIENT, RELATIONSHIP TO DEBTOR	DATE AND PURPOSE OF WITHDRAWAL	AMOUNT OF MONEY OR DESCRIPTION AND VALUE OF PROPERTY

* * * * * *

Appendix A

I declare under penalty of perjury that I have read the answers contained in the foregoing statement of financial affairs and any attachments thereto and that they are true and correct.

Date _____   Signature _____
                                 of Debtor

Date _____   Signature _____
                                 of Joint Debtor
                                 (if any)

*   *   *   *   *   *

I, declare under penalty of perjury that I have read the answers contained in the foregoing statement of financial affairs and any attachments thereto and that they are true and correct to the best of my knowledge, information and belief.

Date _____   Signature _____

                                 _____
                                 Print Name and Title

[An individual signing on behalf of a partnership or corporation must indicate position or relationship to debtor.]

_____ continuation sheets attached

Penalty for making a false statement: Fine of up to $500,000 or imprisonment for up to 5 years, or both. 18 U.S.C. § 152 and 3571

Form B8
6/90

Form 8. CHAPTER 7 INDIVIDUAL DEBTOR'S STATEMENT OF INTENTION

[Caption as in Form 16B]

CHAPTER 7 INDIVIDUAL DEBTOR'S STATEMENT OF INTENTION

1. I, the debtor, have filed a schedule of assets and liabilities which includes consumer debts secured by property of the estate.

2. My intention with respect to the property of the estate which secures those consumer debts is as follows:

    a. *Property to Be Surrendered.*

Description of Property	Creditor's name
1. _____	_____
2. _____	_____
3. _____	_____

    b. *Property to Be Retained. [Check applicable statement of debtor's intention concerning reaffirmation, redemption, or lien avoidance.]*

Description of property	Creditor's name	Debt will be reaffirmed pursuant to § 524(c)	Property is claimed as exempt and will be redeemed pursuant to § 722	Lien will be avoided pursuant to § 522(f) and property will be claimed as exempt
1. _____	_____	_____	_____	_____
2. _____	_____	_____	_____	_____
3. _____	_____	_____	_____	_____
4. _____	_____	_____	_____	_____
5. _____	_____	_____	_____	_____

3. I understand that § 521(2)(B) of the Bankruptcy Code requires that I perform the above stated intention within 45 days of the filing of this statement with the court, or within such additional time as the court, for cause, within such 45-day period fixes.

Date: _____

                                          Signature of Debtor

Appendix B

Computing Net Worth

It is important to understand your financial position before you consider bankruptcy, or indeed, any significant change in your financial relationships.

This appendix will help you to make up a personal balance sheet. It will tell you if you have more assets than liabilities, in which case you may have more flexibility in financial planning.

After you have completed the balance sheet, turn to appendix A and use schedules I and J to figure out exactly where your money is coming from and where it is going.

Who Are "You"?

We are interested in determining the assets and liabilities of the person who is considering the possibility of filing a bankruptcy petition. If you are single, "you," in the following sections, simply means you. If you are married, and the debts with which you are concerned are mostly the responsibility of both of you, then "you" will mean *both of you*. There are cases where it is better for only one spouse to file bankruptcy. This is often true when one spouse has run up the great bulk of the debts, such as in an individual business, and the other spouse is not involved in the business and has not signed any guarantees of business debt. Or it might be because of a judgment against one spouse in an accident case. Your bankruptcy lawyer will be the best judge of that. For purposes of "adding it all up," the aim of this chapter, married couples should prepare the information collectively, as a unit.

Preparing the Personal Balance Sheet

It is necessary for you to gather all of your financial information. If there are things you don't know, and cannot find out after reasonable efforts, you'll have to make your best guess about them.

While it isn't the most efficient way to operate, for most people it is easier to look through the listing quickly, to see what is involved, and then go through it more carefully and gather the information necessary as you get to each line. At the end of the form you'll find notes, tied to the line numbers in the form, which may help you to complete the data. When you get to the end, you'll have a good idea of your net worth.

Think about each item, and put a zero on the line if you don't have a number to enter.

Personal Balance Sheet as of / /19___

Columns

	A	B	C
1 Real property – market value		_____	
2 Mortgages and deeds of trust	_____		
3 Attachments and other liens	_____		
4 Property taxes owing	_____		
5 IRS and other tax liens	_____		
6 Total lines 2 through 5		_____	
7 Line 1 less line 6			_____
8 Cash on hand			_____
9 Checking, savings accounts			_____
10 Security deposits			_____
11 Household furnishings, etc.		_____	
12 Money owed on household furnishings		_____	
13 Line 11 less line 12			_____
14 Life Insurance – cash surrender value		_____	
15 Policy loans		_____	
16 Line 14 less line 15			_____
17 Stocks		_____	
18 Broker or other loans against shares		_____	
19 Line 17 less line 18			_____
20 Partnership interests		_____	
21 Loans against such interests		_____	
22 Line 20 less line 21			_____
23 Bonds	_____		
24 Notes payable to you	_____		

	A	B	C
25 Lines 23 plus line 24		———	
26 Loans against bonds and notes		———	
27 Line 25 less line 26			———
28 Accounts receivable			———
29 Alimony, support due to you (if collectible)			———
30 Other money due to you (realistic value)			———
31 Claims against others (if you can value)			———
32 Patents and copyrights (market value)			———
33 Licenses, franchise agreements, etc. (market value)			———
34 Automobiles, trucks, trailers, etc.		———	
35 Loans against these		———	
36 Line 34 less line 35			———
37 Office equipment, supplies	———		
38 Machinery, fixtures	———		
39 Inventory	———		
40 Total lines 37, 38, 39			———
41 Loans against these		———	
42 Line 40 less line 41			———
43 Farm animals	———		
44 Crops — current value	———		
45 Farming equip. & implements	———		
46 Farm supplies and feed	———		
47 Total lines 43 through 46			———
48 Loans against these		———	

		A	B	C
49	Line 47 less line 48			___
50	Other personal property — market value			___
51	TOTAL ASSETS NET OF SECURED CLAIMS (Total Column C)			___
52	*Priority creditors*			
53	Federal income tax payable	___		
54	State income tax payable	___		
55	"100% penalty" for business taxes	___		
56	Total lines 53 through 55			___
57	Wages due to employees	___		
58	Amounts payable for employee benefits	___		
59	Consumer deposits (up to $900 each)	___		
60	Total lines 53 through 59			___
61	Unsecured ("General") creditors			___
62	NET WORTH (Line 51 less Lines 56, 60, and 61)			___

Notes for Preparing Personal Balance Sheet

Line 1: "Real property" includes the usual kinds of ownership of real estate, as well as condominiums, cooperative apartments, and most time share units. Leased real estate where you are the tenant is not included.

If you own more than one parcel of real estate, it is probably easier to go through the form using totals. This is because many mortgages, liens, etc., may affect more than one property. It can get a bit confusing if you try to divide it up — it's also legally inappropriate in many cases.

It is often very difficult to determine the current value of real estate. If you have owned the property for more than a very short time, your cost is probably not an accurate measure of value. You don't have to be precise in ascribing value; just put down a reasonable estimate. If you have no idea of the value of the property, you should get help from a local broker to figure it out.

In most communities, the value placed on the property by the tax assessor is at best only an outdated estimate of what the property would bring on the current market. Most judges do not admit tax assessors' valuations as evidence of the worth of property.

If other properties like yours have sold recently and you know the prices, you can use them for a guide, adding or subtracting for the differences in the location and improvements.

Short of that, you'll need expert help. We recommend that you find a broker you would use if you decided to sell your property and ask for help on this basis: "My property is not for sale right now. Whether I will sell depends upon what I can reasonably expect to get for it. If I should decide to sell, you will get the listing. In the meantime I need an approximate value for the property. What would you charge me for an oral appraisal?" Since an experienced broker can come up with an approximate value very easily, many would be glad to provide the information either free or for a nominal fee as against your promise of a possible future listing.

If you own property where someone other than your spouse has an interest, list only the value of your share. For example, if you and your brother inherited a house in equal shares, your interest is 50 percent, and only half the value should be included.

Line 2: You can get current mortgage balances from the monthly statements you receive, or by checking the coupon book you use to make payments.

Line 3: Attachments and other liens are claims against your real estate obtained by someone who is suing you. It is important to know if the person suing has a lien on property and is simply suing you for money. The lien is not automatic — there should be something in the papers with which you were served to tell you if the court authorized a lien or attachment. Some kinds of liens, such as liens for persons who worked on your property, can be placed on the property without a court order, but that is not true in every state. If you are represented by an attorney, he or she will know the answer to this question.

The value of the attachment or lien is the amount you reasonably expect to be ordered to pay to the person who is suing you.

Line 4: This line covers only taxes on the real estate that you have listed. Tax liens filed by IRS or state or local authorities go on line 5. Income and other taxes for which no lien has arisen are listed at lines 53-55. These distinctions may become important if you file for bankruptcy.

If you pay your real estate taxes directly, you'll have a recent bill to tell you how much is due. Don't forget interest and penalties if you are late; they can be substantial.

Line 8: This really means cash. If money is in a bank account it goes on line 9.

Line 9: Checking, savings, or other financial accounts; certificates of deposit; or shares in banks or savings and loan, thrift, building and loan, and homestead associations, or credit unions, brokerage houses, or cooperatives. The kind of "shares" mentioned here are really savings or other accounts with various kinds of thrift institutions. "Shares" of the kind traded on stock markets go on line 17. Bonds, government and corporate, go on line 23.

Line 10: Security deposits with public utilities, telephone companies, landlords, and others.

Line 11: Household goods and furnishings, including audio, video, and computer equipment. Include books, pictures, and other art objects; antiques; and stamp, coin, record, tape, compact disc, and other collections or collectibles. Don't forget (if they have any value) wearing apparel; furs and jewelry; and firearms and sports, photographic, and other hobby equipment.

Line 14: You can figure out the cash surrender value of a life insurance policy from the tables that appear at the back. It is a bit of a pain in the neck. If your policy is a "term" policy, it probably has no cash value.

Line 24: This line is for money owed to you for which you have a promissory note or IOU payable to you.

Appendix C

Federal and State Exemption Statutes

FEDERAL EXEMPTIONS

Note: The federal exemptions are available to you only if the proper place for you to file your petition is one of these states:

Connecticut
District of Columbia
Hawaii
Massachusetts
Michigan
Minnesota
New Jersey
New Mexico
Pennsylvania
Rhode Island
Texas
Vermont
Washington
Wisconsin

In these states you can choose either the following federal exemptions or the appropriate state exemptions. It is all or nothing. You cannot pick some federal exemptions and some state exemptions. If husband and wife file jointly, they must agree on which exemption to adopt.

Alimony
    Alimony, child support needed for support.

Homestead

> Real property or mobile home or cooperative used as a residence, up to $7,500.

Insurance

> Unmatured life insurance contract.
> Life insurance policy with loan value up to $4,000.
> Disability, illness or unemployment benefits.
> Life insurance payments for person you depended upon as needed for support.

Pensions

> ERISA-qualified needed for support.

Personal Property

> Motor vehicle to $1,200.
> Animals, crops, clothing, appliances, books, furnishings, household goods, musical instruments to $200 per item; $4,000 total.
> Jewelry to $500.
> Health aids.
> Wrongful death recoveries to $7,500, not including pain and suffering and pecuniary loss.
> Lost-earnings payments.

Public Benefits

> Unemployment compensation, Social Security benefits, others.

Tools of the Trade

> Implements, books, and trade tools to $750.

Wild Card

> Any property to $400; $3,750 in any property less any amount of homestead exemption.

ALABAMA
(Federal exemptions CANNOT be used)

Homestead

> Real property or mobile home value to $5,000; maximum 160 acres; double for married couple.

Insurance

> Life insurance proceeds if spouse or child is beneficiary, or if policy has spendthrift clause re beneficiary.
> Mutual aid and fraternal benefit society benefits.
> Disability proceeds to average of $250 a month.
> Annuity proceeds; maximum $250 a month.

Partnership Property

> Property of business partnership except as against partnership debts.

Pensions

> Judges, law enforcement officers, state employees, teachers.

Personal Property

> $3,000 plus books; burial place; church pew; necessary clothing; family portraits or pictures; arms, uniforms, and equipment that state military personnel are required to keep.

Public Benefits

> Unemployment compensation, workers' compensation, others.

Unpaid Wages

> Earned but unpaid to 75 percent; re consumer loans and credit sales, greater of 75 percent of weekly disposable earnings or thirty times federal minimum hourly wage.

ALASKA

(Federal exemptions CANNOT be used)

Alimony
Alimony and separate maintenance payments.
Child support payments made by collection agency.

Homestead
$54,000 maximum for married couple filing jointly.

Insurance
Disability fraternal benefit society, medical benefits.
Life insurance or annuity either unmatured or to maximum $10,000 in loan value; if beneficiary is insured's spouse or dependent, to extent of wage exemption.
Insurance proceeds for personal injury or wrongful death, to extent wages are exempt.

Miscellaneous
Liquor licenses
Permits for limited entry into Alaska Fisheries

Partnership Property
Partner's interest in partnership property except as a claim against the partnership.

Pensions
ERISA-qualified benefits deposited more than 120 days before filing for bankruptcy.
Teachers and public employees (only benefits building up), to extent wages exempt.

Personal Property
Up to $3,000 in books, musical instruments, clothing, family portraits, household goods, and heirlooms; implements, books, and tools of trade to value of $2,800; building mate-

rials used for repairs or improvements; burial plot; health aids needed for work or to sustain health; jewelry worth up to $1,000; Up to $3,000 in equity in vehicle not worth more than $20,000; personal injury recoveries to extent wages are exempt, except funds to pay medical expenses; pets worth not more than $1,000; proceeds for damaged exempt property; wrongful death recoveries to extent wages are exempt.

Public Benefits

Unemployment compensation, workers' compensation (except to extent of claim for child support), general relief assistance, 45 percent of permanent fund dividends, others.

Unpaid Wages

Weekly net to $350 ($550 for sole wage-earner in household). If pay other than weekly, $1,400 in any month ($2,200 if sole wage-earner).

ARIZONA
(Federal exemptions CANNOT be used)

Homestead

Real property, an apartment, or a mobile home to a value of $100,000 in which debtor resides. Sale proceeds exempt until earlier of purchase of new home or eighteen months after sale. No doubling for married couple.

Insurance

Life insurance proceeds to $20,000 (spouse or child); cash value to $1,000 per dependent ($5,000 maximum).

Group life and fraternal benefit society benefits or proceeds.

Health, accident, or disability benefits except for accrued premiums, debts secured by pledge of policy, and debts paid under policy.

Partnership Property

Partner's interest in specific partnership property.

Pensions

ERISA-qualified benefits deposited more than 120 days before bankruptcy filing; IRAs (by lower court decision); many public employees and elected/appointed officials.

Personal Property

Two beds and living room chair; one dresser, table, lamp, set of bedding per bed; kitchen table; dining room table and four chairs (one more per person); living room carpet or rug; couch; three lamps; three coffee or end tables; pictures, paintings, or drawings created by debtor; family portraits; refrigerator; stove; television, radio or stereo; alarm clock; washer; dryer; vacuum cleaner -- all to total value of $4,000. Bible; bicycle; sewing machine; typewriter; burial plot; rifle, pistol, or shotgun -- all to total value of $500. Books to $250; clothing ($500); wedding and engagement rings ($1,000); watch ($100); pets, horses, milk cows, and poultry ($500); musical instruments ($250); protheses; wheelchair. Food and fuel to last six months; motor vehicle to $1,500, or $4,000 if disabled. Arms, uniforms, etc., required to be kept. Farm machinery, utensils, seed, instruments of husbandry, feed grain, and animals ($2,500 maximum). Teaching aids of teacher; tools, equipment, instruments, and related books to maximum of $2,500, except cannot include vehicle driven to work. Prepaid rent or security deposit to lesser of $1,000 or one and one-half times rent (if homestead not taken). Bank deposit to $150 in one account. Proceeds of sale of damaged exempt property. Married couple may double.

Public Benefits

Unemployment compensation, except if funds are commingled or for debts for necessaries or child support, workers' compensation, welfare benefits.

Unpaid Wages

Seventy-five percent or earned (including pension payments) or earnings in excess of thirty times the federal minimum wage; minor child's earnings, unless debt is for child.

Appendix C

ARKANSAS

(Federal exemptions CANNOT be used)

Homestead (No. 1 or No. 2 as applicable)

No. 1. Head of family: Real or personal property used as residence, value not limited, but acreage and value limitations apply depending upon location of homestead.

No. 2. Real or personal property used as residence: maximum $800 if single; $1250 if married. (See "Personal Property.")

Insurance

Disability and fraternal society benefits; annuity contract.

Cash value of various policies, perhaps limited to $500.

Life insurance proceeds.

Partnership Property

Property of a business partnership.

Pensions

ERISA-qualified plans; certain public employees.

Personal Property

Implements, books and tools of trade up to $750.

Burial plot up to 5 acres, if Homestead No. 2 not taken.

Two hundred dollars ($500 if married or head of family) plus clothing, motor vehicle worth not more than $1,200, wedding band (diamond not to exceed one-half carat).

Public Benefits

Unemployment compensation if not commingled and except for necessaries during period of unemployment; workers' compensation except for child support claims; others.

Unpaid Wages

Not exceeding $25 per week.

Appendix C

CALIFORNIA
(Federal exemptions CANNOT be used)

IMPORTANT NOTE: California has two different systems of exemptions — you must choose No. 1 or No. 2

System No. 1

Homestead

Real or personal property occupied as residence at the time of filing bankruptcy, including mobile home, boat, cooperative stock, community apartment, planned development or condo, and proceeds (including homeowners' insurance proceeds) of any of the above for six months after receipt.

Dollar limitations

$50,000 if single and not disabled.

$75,000 for families (one per family)

$100,000 if:

- 65 or older;
- physically or mentally disabled;
- 55 or older, single and earn less than $15,000
- 55 or older, married and earn less than $20,000

(In last two cases, creditors must be seeking to force sale of home)

Insurance

Fraternal life (to $4,000 loan value) or unemployment benefits.

Matured life insurance benefits needed for support.

Unmatured life insurance polices to $4,000 loan value.

Life insurance proceeds with spendthrift clause.

Disability or health insurance benefits.

Fidelity bonds.

Miscellaneous
Licenses other than liquor licenses (business or professional); inmate trust funds to $1,000.

Partnership Property
Property of business partnership.

Pensions
Private retirement benefits; IRAs and Keogh plans; public and county employees.

Personal Property
Motor vehicles not used in trade to $1,200 in value, or insurance proceeds in that amount of damaged or lost.
Necessary appliances, furnishings, clothing and food.
Tools, implements, materials, instruments, uniforms, books, furnishings, equipment, vessel, motor vehicle used in trade (maximum $2,500 - $5,000 if both spouses use for work).
Bank deposits from Social Security payments.
Building materials to repair or improve home (maximum $1,000); burial plot; health aids; $2,500 in jewelry, heirlooms and art; personal injury and wrongful death causes of action and recoveries needed for support.

Public Benefits
Unemployment compensation, workers' compensation, others.

Wages
Seventy-five percent paid within thirty days of filing.

System No. 2

Alimony

Alimony and child support needed for support.

Homestead or Burial Plot

Real or personal property, including cooperative, used as residence, or burial plot, value not over $7,500. If not used for homestead, can be applied to any property.

Insurance

Unmatured life insurance contract and cash value to $4,000.

Disability benefits.

Life insurance proceeds needed for support of family.

Pensions

ERISA-qualified needed for support.

Personal Property

Motor vehicle ($1,200); animals, crops, appliances, furnishings, household goods, books, musical instruments, and clothing up to $200 per item; jewelry ($500); health aids; personal injury recoveries, not to include pain and suffering ($7,500 maximum); wrongful death recoveries needed for support; the unused portion of homestead or burial exemption, plus $400, may be used on any property.

Public Benefits

Unemployment compensation, public assistance, Social Security, crime victims' compensation, veterans' benefits.

Appendix C

COLORADO

(Federal Exemptions CANNOT be used)

Homestead

Real property occupied when file bankruptcy to value of $20,000. Same re mobile home or manufactured home if debt incurred after January 1, 1983 (earlier was $3,500 for house trailer or coach, $6,000 for mobile home). Sale proceeds exempt one year after received if kept separately or used for new residence.

Insurance

Group life policy or proceeds; all life insurance proceeds if spendthrift clause.

Disability insurance lump sum payment, or up to $200 per month except for debts for necessaries.

Fraternal benefit society benefits.

Homeowner's insurance proceeds for one year after received; maximum $20,000.

Partnership Property

Property of a business partnership.

Pensions

ERISA-qualified and IRAs, to the extent wages are exempt; public employees.

Personal Property

Clothing valued at up to $750; one burial plot each for debtor and dependents; food and fuel ($300); health aids; household goods ($1500); jewelry ($500); motor vehicles ($1,000 for commuting; $3,000 to get medical care if elderly or disabled); horses, mules, wagons, carts machinery, harness, and tools of farmer ($2,000); livestock and poultry of farmer ($3,000); library of professional ($1,500); stock in trade, supplies, fixtures, machines, tools, maps, equipment, and books ($1,500); personal injury recoveries unless debt related to injury; pictures and books ($750); proceeds of damaged exempt property; security deposit.

Public Benefits

Unemployment compensation; workers' compensation, others.

Unpaid Wages

Greater of 75 percent of disposable earnings or thirty times federal minimum hourly wage.

CONNECTICUT
(Federal exemption ARE available)

Alimony and child support
> Alimony to the extent wages are exempt and child support.

Insurance
> Health or disability benefits.
> Benefits under no-fault insurance law except for court ordered support payments.
> Life insurance proceeds.

Partnership Property
> Property of a business partnership.

Pensions
> ERISA-qualified; state and municipal employees.

Personal Property
> Necessary appliances, furniture, bedding, health aids, food and clothing; burial plot; motor vehicle to value of $1,500; arms, military equipment, uniforms and musical instruments of military personnel; necessary tools, books, instruments and farm animals; proceeds of damaged exempt property; residential utility and security deposits for one residence; wedding and engagement rings.

Unpaid Wages
> Wages exempt except for lesser of 25 percent of weekly wages or excess over 40 times federal hourly minimum wage. Exempt wages may be reached for court ordered support.

Appendix C

DELAWARE

(Federal exemptions CANNOT be used)

Overall
Single person not more than $5,000; husband and wife not more than $10,000.

Insurance
Life insurance proceeds.
Health, disability, fraternal, employee life, benefits.
Annuity proceeds to $350 a month

Partnership Property
Property of a business partnership.

Pensions
State, Kent County employees; police officers and volunteer firefighters.

Personal Property
Five hundred dollars of any except tools of trade (if head of family); Bible, books, and family pictures; burial plot; church pew or equivalent; tools of trade to $50 or $75 depending on county; clothing, including jewelry; pianos; leased organs and sewing machines.

Public Benefits
Unemployment compensation, except for child support and necessaries and, so long as not commingled, workers' compensation, others.

Unpaid Wages
Eighty-five percent.

Appendix C

DISTRICT OF COLUMBIA
(Federal exemptions ARE available)

Tenancy by the Entirety
May be exempt where debt only of one spouse.

Insurance
Life insurance proceeds (including group and group policy).
Disability and fraternal benefit society benefits.
Minor amounts of other insurance proceeds.

Partnership Property
Property of a business partnership.

Pensions
Judges, public school teachers. See "unpaid wages" below.

Personal Property
Household goods to $300 total; books to $400, clothing per family member to $300; library, furniture, tools, of professional or artist to $300; tools of trade or business to $200; motor vehicle, cart, etc., used in debtor's business; stock and materials to $200; family pictures; food and fuel for three months; residential condominium deposit.

Public Benefits
Unemployment compensation, workers' compensation, others.

Unpaid Wages
Seventy-five percent, including pension payments or thirty times federal minimum hourly wage; nonwage for sixty days at $200 per month for head of family, otherwise $60 per month.

FLORIDA

(Federal exemptions CANNOT be used)

Alimony
> Alimony, child support to the extent needed for support.

Homestead
> Real property, mobile or modular home or condominium to unlimited value; property cannot exceed one-half acre in municipality or 160 contiguous acres in other places.
> Property held as tenants by the entirety may be exempt against debts owed by only one spouse.

Insurance
> Annuity contract proceeds.
> Disability or illness benefits.
> Fraternal benefit society benefits, if received before October 1, 1996.
> Life insurance cash surrender value.
> Death benefits payable to a specific beneficiary.

Miscellaneous
> Monies paid into or out of prepaid Post-Secondary Education Expense Trust Fund exempt against claims against the purchaser or beneficiary.

Partnership Property
> Property of a business partnership.

Pensions
> ERISA-qualified benefits, county officers and employees, firefighters, highway patrol officers, police officers, state officers and employees, teachers.

Personal Property
> Any personal property to $1,000

Public Benefits

> Unemployment compensation, except for child support obligations, workers' compensation, veterans' benefits, others.

Unpaid Wages

> Earned but unpaid or paid and in bank account.
>
> Federal government employees' pension payments needed for support and received three months before filing for bankruptcy.

Appendix C

GEORGIA
(Federal exemptions CANNOT be used)

Alimony
> Alimony and child support necessary for support.

Homestead
> Real or personal property, including cooperative, used as a residence to $5,000 per debtor. Unused portion may be applied to any other property.

Insurance
> Annuity and endowment contract benefits.
> Disability or health benefits to $250 per month.
> Fraternal benefit society benefits.
> Group insurance.
> Industrial life insurance proceeds and life insurance proceeds if policy is owned by someone you depended on and is needed for support.
> Life insurance proceeds or avails if beneficiary is not the insured.
> Unmatured life insurance contract other than credit life insurance.
> Unmatured life insurance dividends, interest, loan or cash value to $2,000, if beneficiary is the debtor or someone the debtor depended upon.

Pensions
> ERISA-qualified benefits, public employees, pensions needed for support.

Personal Property
> Animals, crops, clothing, appliances, books, furnishings, household goods, musical instruments to $200 per item; burial plot in lieu of homestead; health aids; jewelry to

$500; motor vehicles to $1,000; lost future earnings needed for support; personal injury recoveries to $7,500; wrongful death recoveries needed for support; $400 in any item and the unused portion of the homestead exemption.

Public Benefits

Unemployment compensation, workers' compensation, social security benefits, veterans' benefits, others.

Tools of the Trade

Implements, books and trade tools to $500.

Unpaid Wages

The greater of 75 percent of earned but unpaid wages for private and federal workers, or thirty times the federal minimum hourly wage.

HAWAII
(Federal exemptions ARE available)

Homestead
> Real property to $20,000, except for head of family or debtor over 65 to $30,000; property cannot exceed one acre; sale proceeds exempt for six months after sale; property held as tenancy by the entirety may be exempt against debts owed by only one spouse.

Insurance
> Annuity contract or endowment policy proceeds if beneficiary is insured's spouse, child or parent.
> Disability benefits.
> Fraternal benefit society benefits.
> Group life insurance policy or proceeds.
> Life or health insurance policy for spouse or child.
> Life insurance proceeds if proceeds cannot be used to pay beneficiary's creditors.

Partnership Property
> Property of business partnership.

Pensions
> ERISA-qualified benefits deposited three years prior to filing; firefighters, police officers, public officers and employees.

Personal Property
> Appliances and furnishings, books, burial plot to 250 square feet plus tombstone, monuments and fencing on site, clothing, housing down payment for home in state project, jewelry and the like to $1,000, motor vehicle to wholesale value of $1,000, proceeds for sold or damaged exempt

property, sale proceeds from exempt property for six months after sale.

Public Benefits
Unemployment compensation except for child support, workers' compensation, others.

Tools of Trade
Tools, implements, books, instruments, uniforms, furnishings, fishing boat, nets, motor vehicle and other personal property needed for work.

Unpaid Wages
Unpaid wages for services performed for past thirty-one days (after thirty-one days, 95 percent of the first $100, 90 percent of second $100, and 80 percent of balance), prisoners' wages.

Appendix C

IDAHO
(Federal exemptions CANNOT be used)

Alimony
> Alimony and child support necessary for support and as long as funds are not commingled.

Homestead
> Real property or mobile home to $30,000; sale proceeds are exempt of six months.

Insurance
> Annuity contract proceeds to $350 per month.
> Death or disability benefits.
> Fraternal benefit society benefits.
> Group life insurance benefits.
> Life insurance proceeds if proceeds are prohibited from being used to pay beneficiary's creditors.
> Life insurance proceeds for beneficiary other than the insured.
> Medical benefits.
> Others.

Miscellaneous
> Liquor licenses.

Partnership Property
> Property of a business partnership.

Pensions
> ERISA-qualified benefits; firefighters, police officers, public employees, other pensions needed for support as received and as long as payments are not commingled with other money.

Personal Property

Appliances, furnishings, books, clothing, musical instruments, pets, family portraits and heirlooms, and one firearm up to $500 per item and up to $4,000 total; building materials for construction and repairs; burial plot for debtor and family; crops cultivated by debtor on a maximum plot of fifty acres to $1,000, including water rights of 160 inches; health aids; jewelry to $250; motor vehicle to $1,500; personal injury recoveries need for support so long as funds are not commingled; wrongful death recoveries to the extent needed for support; proceeds for damage to exempt property for three months after receipt.

Public Benefits

Unemployment compensation except for debts incurred for necessities; workers' compensation, veterans' benefits, others.

Tools of the Trade

Arms, uniforms, and other equipment required for peace officers, national guardsmen and military personnel; implements, books and trade tools to $1,000.

Unpaid Wages

Earned but unpaid wages exempt except as to the lesser of 25 percent of disposable income or amount in excess of thirty times the federal minimum hourly wage, subject to child support obligations.

Appendix C

ILLINOIS
(Federal exemptions CANNOT be used)

Alimony
> Alimony and child support needed for support.

Homestead
> Real or personal property, including a farm, lot and build-
> ings, condominium, cooperative or mobile home to
> $7,500; sale proceeds are exempt for one year; spouse or
> child of deceased owner may claim homestead; husband
> and wife may double.

Insurance
> Fraternal benefit society benefits.
> Health or disability benefits.
> Homeowners proceeds if home is destroyed to $7,500.
> Life insurance or annuity proceeds or cash value if the ben-
> eficiary is the insured's child, parent, spouse, or other de-
> pendent.
> Life insurance policy if the beneficiary is the insured's wife
> or child.
> Life insurance proceeds if proceeds cannot be used to pay
> beneficiary's creditors and if needed for support.

Partnership Property
> Property of a business partnership.

Pensions
> Civil service employees, county employees, disabled fire-
> fighters and widows and children of firefighters, firefight-
> ers, general assembly members, house of correction em-
> ployees, judges, municipal employees, park employees,
> police officers, public library employees, sanitation district
> employees, state employees, state university employees,

teachers; ERISA-qualified benefits as to payments being received.

Personal Property

Bible, family pictures, school books, health aids, clothing needed, motor vehicle to $1,200, personal injury recoveries to $7,500, proceeds of sold exempt property, wrongful death recoveries of an individual on whom the debtor was dependent to the extent necessary for support, and up to $2,000 in any personal property, including wages.

Public Benefits

Unemployment compensation, except for certain child support claims, veterans' benefits, workers' compensation, others.

Tools of the Trade

Implements, books and trade tools to $750.

Unpaid Wages

Lesser of 85 percent of weekly disposable wages or forty times the federal minimum wage.

INDIANA
(Federal exemptions CANNOT be used)

Homestead
> Real or personal property used as a residence to $7,500.
> Homestead plus personal property, excluding health aids cannot exceed $10,000; property held as tenants by the entirety may be exempt against debts incurred by only one spouse.

Insurance
> Fraternal benefit society benefits.
> Group life insurance policy.
> Life insurance policy, proceeds, cash value or avails if the beneficiary is the insured's spouse or dependent.
> Life insurance proceeds if proceeds cannot be used to pay beneficiary's creditors.
> Mutual life or accident proceeds.

Partnership Property
> Property of a business partnership.

Pensions
> Firefighters, police officers, public employees, public or private retirement benefits, sheriffs, state teachers.

Personal Property
> Health aids, up to $4,000 of any nonresidential real estate or tangible personal property, up to $100 of any intangible personal property except money owed to the debtor.

Public Benefits
> Unemployment compensation, workers' compensation except one-half may go to child support, others.

Tools of the Trade
> National guard uniforms, arms and equipment.

Unpaid Wages
> Minimum of 75 percent of earned but unpaid wages.

Appendix C

IOWA
(Federal exemptions CANNOT be used)

Alimony
> Alimony and child support to the extent needed for support.

Homestead
> Real property or an apartment to an unlimited value; property cannot exceed one-half acre in town or city or forty acres elsewhere, except that the amount may be increased to obtain a value of $500.

Insurance
> Accident, disability, health, illness, or life insurance proceeds or avails to $15,000, if paid to surviving spouse, child, or other dependent.
> Employee group insurance policy or proceeds.
> Life insurance proceeds up to $10,000, acquired within two years of filing, paid to spouse, child, or other dependent.
> Life insurance proceeds if proceeds cannot be used to pay the beneficiary's creditors.

Partnership Property
> Property of a business partnership.

Pensions
> Disabled firefighters, police officers (payments being received), federal government pensions (payments being received), firefighters, peace officers, police officers, public employees, other pensions needed for support.

Personal Property
> Appliances, furnishings, and household goods up to $2,000 total; bank deposit of up to $100 or $100 in cash; Bibles,

books, portraits, libraries, pictures, and paintings up to
$1,000 total; burial plot to one acre; clothing up to $1,000;
health aids; motor vehicle, musical instruments; and tax re-
funds, up to $5,000 total, except tax refund may not exceed
$1,000; rifle, musket, or shotgun; wedding or engagement
rings.

Public Benefits

Unemployment compensation, veterans' benefits, workers'
compensation, others.

Tools of the Trade

Farming equipment, including livestock, feed up to
$10,000; nonfarming equipment up to $10,000; cannot include car.

Unpaid Wages

Exempt except for $250 per creditor per year, subject to
statutory formula; all earnings between $12,000 and
$16,000, except to the extent of $400; between $16,000
and $24,000, except to the extent of $800; between
$24,000 and $35,000, except to the extent of $1,500; be-
tween $35,000 and $50,000, except to the extent of $2,000;
all earnings in excess of $50,000, except to the extent of
not more than 10 percent.

Appendix C

KANSAS
(Federal exemptions CANNOT be used)

Homestead

Real property or mobile home to unlimited value; property cannot exceed one acre in incorporated town or 160 acres on farm; property must be occupied or intended to be occupied at time of filing.

Insurance

Fraternal life insurance benefits.

Life insurance forfeiture value if bankruptcy filing occurs over one year from issuance of policy.

Life insurance proceeds if proceeds cannot be used to pay beneficiary's creditors.

Life insurance proceeds up to $1,000, payable to deceased's estate, not to a specific beneficiary.

Life insurance proceeds or cash value deposited into bank account.

Miscellaneous

Liquor licenses.

Partnership Property

Property of a business partnership.

Pensions

ERISA-qualified benefits; elected and appointed official in cities with populations between 120,000 and 200,000; federal government pensions to the extent needed for support and paid within three months of filing (only payments being received); firefighters; judges; police officers; public employees; state highway patrol officers; state school employees.

PERSONAL BANKRUPTCY

Personal Property

Burial plot or crypt, clothing to last one year, food and fuel to last one year, furnishings and household equipment, jewelry, and the like up to $1,000, motor vehicle up to $20,000 (no limit is vehicle is designed for disabled or handicapped).

Public Benefits

Unemployment compensation, workers' compensations, others.

Tools of the Trade

Books, documents, furniture, instruments, equipment, breeding stock, seed, grain, and stock up to $7,500 in total.

Unpaid Wages

The greater of 75 percent of earned but unpaid wages or thirty times the federal minimum wage.

KENTUCKY
(Federal exemptions CANNOT be used)

Alimony
>Alimony and child support as needed for support.

Homestead
>Real or personal property used as a residence up to $5,000 for debts incurred after purchase; sale proceeds are exempt. An additional $1,000 can be applied to the homestead, if not used for personalty.

Insurance
>Annuity contract proceeds up to $350 per month.
>Cooperative life or casualty insurance benefits.
>Fraternal benefit society benefits.
>Group life insurance proceeds.
>Life insurance proceeds if proceeds cannot be used to pay beneficiary's creditors.
>Life insurance proceeds or cash value if beneficiary is someone other than the insured.

Partnership Property
>Property of a business partnership.

Pensions
>Firefighters, police officers, state employees, teachers, urban county government employees, other pensions, except as to contributions made within 120 days of the bankruptcy filing.

Personal Property
>Burial plot up to $5,000 in lieu of homestead; clothing, jewelry, and the like and furnishings up to $3,000 in total; health aids; lost-earnings payments needed for support;

medical expenses paid and reparation benefits received under the motor vehicle reparation law; motor vehicle to $2,500; personal injury recoveries to $7,500 (not including pain and suffering or pecuniary loss); wrongful death recoveries for person you depended on as needed for support; up to $1,000 in any property.

Public Benefits

Unemployment compensation as long as it is not commingled and subject to claims for necessities; workers' compensation, others.

Tools of Trade

Library, office equipment, instruments and furnishings of minister, attorney, physician, surgeon, chiropractor, veterinarian, or dentist to $1,000; motor vehicle of mechanic, mechanical or electrical equipment servicer, minister, attorney, physician, surgeon, chiropractor, veterinarian, or dentist to $2,500; tools, equipment, livestock, and poultry of a farmer to $3,000; tools of a nonfarmer to $300.

Unpaid Wages

Minimum of 75 percent of earned but unpaid wages.

Appendix C

LOUISIANA
(Federal exemptions CANNOT be used)

Homestead

 Real property to $15,000; property cannot exceed 160 acres on one tract or on two or more tracts if there is a home on one tract and a field, garden, or pasture on the others; husband and wife may not double; spouse or child of a deceased owner may claim the exemption; spouse given home in a divorce proceeding gets the exemption; homestead must be occupied when the exemption is claimed.

Insurance

 Fraternal benefit society benefits.

 Group insurance policies or proceeds.

 Health, accident or disability proceeds or avails.

 Life insurance proceeds or avails.

 If life insurance, endowment policy or annuity is issued within nine months of the bankruptcy, exemption is limited to $35,000.

Miscellaneous

 Property of minor child.

Pensions

 Gratuitous payments to employee or heirs whenever paid, except as to child support obligations; ERISA-qualified pensions and IRAs are exempt to the extent tax-exempt and if contributions are made more than one year prior to bankruptcy filing.

Personal Property

 Arms, military items, bedding, linens and bedroom furniture, chinaware, glassware, utensils, silverware (not sterling), clothing, family portraits, musical instruments, heating and cooling equipment, living and dining room furniture, poultry, fowl, one cow, pressing irons, sewing machine, refrigerator, freezer, stove, washer and dryer; cemetery plot and monuments; engagement and wedding rings to $5,000; equipment needed for therapy.

Public Benefits

Unemployment compensation if not commingled and except for necessities and support obligations, workers' compensation except for alimony.

Tools of the Trade

Tools, instruments, books, pick-up truck (maximum three tons), or nonluxury automobile and utility trailer needed for work.

Unpaid Wages

The greater of 75 percent of weekly disposable earnings or thirty times the federal minimum wage.

Appendix C

MAINE
(Federal exemptions CANNOT be used)

Alimony

Alimony and child support, 50 percent if supporting spouse or child, otherwise 40 percent.

Homestead

Real or personal property, including cooperative, used as a residence to $7,500; if the debtor is over sixty or physically or mentally disabled to $60,000; joint debtors may double.

Insurance

Annuity proceeds to $450 per month.

Disability or health proceeds, benefits or avails.

Fraternal benefit society benefits.

Group health or life policy or proceeds.

Life, endowment, annuity, or accident policy, proceeds or avails.

Life insurance policy, interest, loan value, or accrued dividends from policy of person you depended on to $4,000.

Unmatured life insurance policy.

Partnership Property

Property of a business partnership.

Pensions

ERISA-qualified pensions; judges, legislators, state employees.

Personal Property

Animals, crops, musical instruments, books to $200 per item; balance due on repossessed goods (total amount financed cannot exceed $2,000); burial plot in lieu of homestead exemption; clothing, furnishings, household goods, appliances, tools of trade (above the tools-of-the-trade exemption), and personal injury recoveries (above personal injury recovery exemption) to $4,500 total (these items may be claimed in lieu of the homestead exemption); cooking stove, furnaces and stoves for heat; food to last six months, fuel not to exceed ten cords of wood, five tons of coal or 1,000 gallons of petroleum; health aids; jewelry (not wedding or engagement rings) to $500; lost-earnings payments needed for support; military clothes, arms, and equipment; motor vehicle to $1,200; personal injury recoveries to $7,500, not including pain and suffering awards; seeds, fertilizer, and feed to raise and harvest food for one season; tools and equipment to raise and harvest food; wedding and engagement rings; wrongful death recoveries needed for support; $400 of any property and unused portion of residence exemption but not exceeding $4,500 in exempt property.

Public Benefits

Unemployment compensation, except for debts incurred for necessities during unemployment, veterans' benefits, workers' compensation, others.

Tools of the Trade

Boat not exceeding five tons used in commercial fishing; books, materials and stock to $1,000; one of each type of farm implement needed to harvest and raise crops.

Unpaid Wages

Exempt except for 25 percent of the amount in excess of forty times the federal minimum hourly wage.

Appendix C

MARYLAND
(Federal exemptions CANNOT be used)

Homestead
> None, except that property held as tenancy by the entirety may be exempt against debts owed by only one spouse.

Insurance
> Disability or health benefits, including court awards, arbitrations, and settlements.
> Fraternal benefit society benefits.
> Life insurance or annuity contract proceeds or avails if beneficiary is insured's dependent, child, or spouse, unless debtor elects to receive dividends in cash.
> Medical benefits deducted from wages.

Partnership Property
> Property of a business partnership.

Pensions
> Deceased Baltimore police officers (only benefits building up), state employees, state police, teachers; ERISA-qualified benefits, except IRAs.

Personal Property
> Appliances, furnishings, household goods, books, pets, and clothing up to $500 total; burial plot; health aids; lost future earnings recoveries; $3,000 in property of any kind plus $2,500 in real or personal property.

Public Benefits
> Unemployment compensation, workers' compensation, others.

Unpaid Wages

Earned but unpaid wages in the greater of 75 percent or $145 per week; in Kent, Caroline, and Queen Anne and Worcester Counties, the greater of 75 percent or actual wages or 30 percent of the federal minimum wage.

Appendix C

MASSACHUSETTS
(Federal exemptions ARE available)

Homestead

Exemption amount is $100,000 ($200,000 for those over 65 or disabled), except with respect to debts arising prior to or for the purchase of the homestead and support; property held as tenants by the entirety may be exempt against non-necessity debts; joint owners may not double; homestead must be occupied or intended to be occupied at the time of filing for bankruptcy; homestead declaration must be recorded prior to filing for bankruptcy; spouse or child of a deceased owner may claim the exemption.

Insurance

Disability benefits to $35 per week.

Fraternal benefit society benefits.

Group annuity policy or proceeds.

Group life insurance policy.

Life or endowment policy, proceeds or cash value.

Life insurance annuity contract that says it is exempt.

Life insurance proceeds if proceeds cannot be used to pay the debts of the beneficiary.

Medical malpractice self-insurance.

Miscellaneous

Moving expenses upon eminent domain taking.

Partnership Property

Property of a business partnership.

Pensions

ERISA-qualified benefits; private retirement benefits, public employees, savings bank employees.

Personal Property

> Bank deposits to $125; food or cash for food to $300; beds, bedding and heating unit; clothing needed; bibles and books to $200 total; sewing machine to $200; burial plots, tombs and church pew; cash for fuel, heat, water or light to $75 per month; cash to $200 per month for rent in lieu of homestead; cooperative association shares to $100; 2 cows, 12 sheep, 2 swine, 4 tons of hay; furniture to $3,000; motor vehicle to $750; trust company, bank or credit union deposits to $500.

Public Benefits

> Unemployment compensation, except as to support obligations, veterans' benefits, workers' compensation except as to support obligations, others.

Tools of the Trade

> Arms, uniforms and other items required for military; boats, fishing tackle and nets of fisherman to $500; material you designed and procured to $500; tools, implements and fixtures to $500 total.

Unpaid Wages

> Earned but unpaid wages to $125 per week; payments (wage or pension) to $100 per week.

MICHIGAN
(Federal exemptions ARE available)

Homestead
> Real property, including condominium to $3,500; property cannot exceed one lot in town, village, or city or forty acres elsewhere; property held as tenancy by the entirety may be exempt against debts owed by only one spouse; spouse or child of deceased owner may claim the exemption.

Insurance
> Disability, mutual life, or health benefits.
> Fraternal benefit society benefits.
> Life, endowment, or annuity proceeds if proceeds cannot be used to pay the beneficiary's creditors.
> Life or endowment proceeds if beneficiary is insured's spouse or child.
> Life insurance proceeds to $300 per year if beneficiary is a married woman or a husband.
> Life insurance or avails.

Partnership Property
> Property of a business partnership.

Pensions
> Firefighters, police officers, judges, legislators, probate judges, public school employees, state employees.
> ERISA-qualified benefits, including IRAs to the extent they are tax-deferred and subject to separate maintenance and child support and not contributed within 120 days of bankruptcy.

Personal Property
> Appliances, utensils, books, furniture, and household goods to $1,000 total; building and loan association shares to

$1,000 par value in lieu of homestead; burial plots, cemeteries; church pew, slip, seat; clothing, family pictures; two cows, one hundred hens, five roosters, ten sheep, five swine; hay and grain to last six months for head of household; food and fuel to last six months for head of household.

Public Benefits

Unemployment compensation, workers' compensation, others.

Tools of the Trade

Arms and accoutrements required for service; tools, implements, materials, stock, apparatus, team, motor vehicle, horse, and harness to $1,000 total.

Unpaid Wages

Sixty percent of earned but unpaid wages for head of household, 40 percent for others; head of household may keep at least $15 per week plus $2 per week for each non-spouse dependent; others may keep at least $10 per week.

Appendix C

MINNESOTA
(Federal exemptions ARE available)

Homestead

Real property, mobile home, or manufactured home to un-limited value; property cannot exceed one-half acre in city or 160 acres elsewhere; proceeds from sale are exempt for one year.

Insurance

Accident or disability proceeds.

Fraternal benefit society benefits.

Life insurance or endowment proceeds or avails if beneficiary is not the insured.

Life insurance proceeds if proceeds cannot be used to pay the beneficiary's creditors.

Life insurance proceeds if the beneficiary is the spouse or child of the insured to $20,000 plus $5,000 per dependent.

Police, fire, or beneficiary association benefits.

Unmatured life insurance contract dividends, interest on loan value to $4,000 if insured is debtor or someone debtor depends upon.

Miscellaneous

Earnings of minor children.

Partnership Property

Property of a business partnership.

Personal Property

Appliances, furniture, radio, phonographs, and television to $4,500 total; Bible, books, and musical instruments; burial plot to 100 acres; church pew or seat; motor vehicle to $2,000; clothing, including watch; food and utensils; personal injury recoveries; proceeds for damaged exempt property; wrongful death recoveries.

Public Benefits

Unemployment compensation as long as funds are not commingled and except for necessities; veteran's benefits, workers' compensation, others.

Tools of the Trade

Tools of the trade, excluding teaching material, cannot exceed $13,000; farm machines, implements, livestock, farm produce, and crops of farmers to $13,000 total; teaching materials, including books and chemical apparatus, of public school teacher; tools, implements, machines, instruments, furniture, stock in trade, and library to $5,000 total.

Unpaid Wages

Earned but unpaid wages, paid within six months of returning to work, if welfare was received in the past; minimum of 75 percent of earned but unpaid wages.

MISSISSIPPI
(Federal exemptions CANNOT be used)

Homestead

Property to $30,000; property cannot exceed 160 acres; sale proceeds are exempt; property must be occupied unless claimant is over sixty and married or widowed.

Insurance

Disability benefits.

Fraternal benefit society benefits.

Homeowners' insurance proceeds to $30,000.

Life insurance policy or proceeds to $50,000.

Life insurance proceeds if proceeds cannot be used to pay beneficiary's creditors.

Life insurance proceeds to $5,000 if beneficiary is deceased's estate, not a specific beneficiary, and proceeds left to pay deceased's debts.

Partnership Property

Property of a business partnership.

Pensions

ERISA-qualified benefits deposited over one year before the bankruptcy filing, including IRAs and Keoghs.

Firefighters, highway patrol officers, police officers, state employees, teachers.

Public employees retirement and disability benefits.

Private retirement benefits to the extent tax-deferred.

Personal Property

Tangible personal property of any kind to $10,000; personal injury judgments to $10,000; proceeds from exempt property.

Public Benefits

Unemployment compensation as long as the funds are not commingled and are subject for debts for necessities, workers' compensation, others.

Unpaid Wages

Earned but unpaid wages owed for thirty days; greater of 75 percent of disposable earnings or thirty times the federal minimum wage.

MISSOURI
(Federal exemptions ARE available)

Alimony
> Alimony and child support to $500 per month.

Homestead
> Real property to $8,000 or mobile home to $1,000; property held as tenancy by the entireties may be exempt from debts owed by only one spouse; joint owners may not double.

Insurance
> Assessment or insurance premium proceeds.
> Death, disability or illness benefits needed for support.
> Fraternal benefit society benefits to $5,000, bought over six months before filing.
> Life insurance dividends, loan value, or interest to $5,000, bought over six months before filing.
> Life insurance proceeds if policy owned by a woman and insures her husband.
> Life insurance proceeds if policy owned by unmarried woman and beneficiary is her father or brother.
> Stipulated insurance premiums.
> Unmatured life insurance policy.

Partnership Property
> Property of a business partnership.

Pensions
> Employees of cities with more than 100,00 people; ERISA-qualified benefits needed for support (only payments being received); firefighters, highway, and transportation employees; police department employees, public officers, and employees; state employees; teachers.

Personal Property
> Appliances, household goods, furnishings, clothing, books, crops, animals, and musical instruments to $1,000 total; burial grounds to one acre or $100; health aids; jewelry to $500; motor vehicle to $500; personal injury cause of action except for support obligations; wrongful death recoveries for person debtor depends upon; $400 in property of any kind; head of household may exempt an additional $850 plus $250 per unmarried dependent.

Public Benefits
> Unemployment compensation, workers' compensation, others.

Unpaid Wages
> Minimum of 75 percent of earned but unpaid wages (90 percent for head of a family); wages of a servant or common laborer to $90.

Appendix C

MONTANA

(Federal exemptions CANNOT be used)

Alimony
>Alimony and child support.

Homestead
>Real property or mobile home to $40,000; sale, condemna-
tion, or insurance proceeds exempt for eighteen months;
property must be occupied at the time of bankruptcy filing;
homestead declaration must be recorded prior to filing.

Insurance
>Annuity contract proceeds to $350 per month.
>Disability or illness proceeds, avails, or benefits; medical,
surgical or hospital care benefits.
>Fraternal benefit society benefits.
>Group life insurance policy or proceeds.
>Hail insurance benefits.
>Life insurance proceeds if proceeds cannot be used to pay
beneficiary's creditors.
>Life insurance proceeds or avails; if annual premiums do not
exceed $500.
>Unmatured life insurance contract to $4,000.

Partnership Property
>Property of a business partnership.

Pensions
>ERISA-qualified benefits deposited over one year before
filing for bankruptcy in excess of 15 percent of debtor's
yearly income; firefighters, game wardens, highway patrol
officers, judges, police officers, public employees, sheriffs,
teachers.

PERSONAL BANKRUPTCY

Personal Property
> Appliances, household furnishings, animals with feed crops, musical instruments, books, firearms, sporting goods, clothing, and jewelry to $600 per item and $4,500 total; burial plot; cooperative association shares to $500 in value; health aids; motor vehicle to $1,200; proceeds for damaged or lost exempt property for six months after receipt.

Public Benefits
> Unemployment compensation except as to child support obligations, workers' compensation except as to medical services related to injury and child support, others.

Tools of the Trade
> Implements, books, and tools of trade to $3,000; uniforms, arms, and accoutrements needed to carry out government functions.

Unpaid Wages
> Greater of 75 percent of disposable earnings or thirty times the federal minimum hourly wage except as to child support.

NEBRASKA
(Federal exemptions CANNOT be used)

Homestead
Property to $10,000; property cannot exceed two lots in city or village or 160 acres elsewhere; sale proceeds are exempt for six months after sale.

Insurance
Disability benefits to $200 per month.
Fraternal benefit society benefits to loan value of $10,000.
Life insurance or annuity contract proceeds to $10,000 loan value.

Partnership Property
Property of a business partnership

Pensions
ERISA-qualified benefits needed for support; county employees, school employees, state employees; military disability benefits to $2,000.

Personal Property
Burial plot, crypts, lots, tombs, niches, vaults; clothing; food and fuel to last six months; furniture and kitchen utensils to $1,500; perpetual care funds; personal injury recoveries; personal possessions; $2,500 in any personal property in lieu of homestead.

Public Benefits
Unemployment compensation if funds are not commingled and subject to necessities and child support, workers' compensation, others.

Tools of the Trade
Equipment or tools to $1,500.

Unpaid Wages

Minimum 85 percent if earned but unpaid wages or pension payments for head of family; 75 percent for all others.

NEVADA

(Federal exemptions CANNOT be used)

Homestead

Real property or mobile home to $95,000; husband and wife may not double; homestead must be recorded before bankruptcy filing; land held in spendthrift trust is exempt.

Insurance

Annuity contract proceeds to $350 per month.

Fraternal benefit society benefits.

Group life or health policy or proceeds.

Health proceeds or avails.

Life insurance policy or proceeds if annual premiums are not over $1,000.

Partnership Property

Property of a business partnership.

Pensions

Public employees

Personal Property

Appliances, household goods, furniture, home and yard equipment, to $3,000 total; one gun; books to $1,500; burial plot if purchase money is held in trust; funeral service contract if money is held in trust; keepsakes and pictures; metal-bearing ores, geological specimens, art curiosities, or paleontological remains; motor vehicle to $1,000.

Public Benefits

Unemployment compensation if funds are not commingled and are subject to debts for necessities, others.

Tools of the Trade

> Arms, uniforms, and accoutrements required for service; cabin or dwelling of miner or prospector; cars, implements, and appliances for mining and mining claim you work to $4,500 total; farm trucks, stock, tools, equipment, and seed to $4,500; library, equipment, supplies, tools, and materials to $4,500.

Unpaid Wages

> Greater of 75 percent of disposable earnings or thirty times the federal minimum wage.

NEW HAMPSHIRE
(Federal exemptions CANNOT be used)

Homestead

Real property or manufactured housing owned and occu-pied by the same person to $5,000; effective January 1, 1993, the exemption amount increases to $30,000.

Insurance

Firefighters' aid insurance.

Fraternal benefit society benefits.

Homeowners' insurance proceeds to $5,000.

Life insurance or endowment proceeds if claimant is not the insured.

Life insurance or endowment proceeds if the beneficiary is a married woman.

Miscellaneous

Child support, jury fees, witness fees, wages of minor chil-dren.

Partnership Property

Property of a business partnership.

Pensions

Federally created pensions (only benefits building up), fire-fighters, police officers, public employees.

Personal Property

Automobile to $1,000; beds, bedsteads, bedding, and cook-ing utensils; Bibles and books to $800; burial plot, lot, church pew; clothing needed; cooking and heating stoves, refrigerator; cow, six sheep or fleece; four tons hay; domes-tic fowl to $300; food and fuel to $400; furniture to $2,000;

hog, pork if slaughtered; jewelry to $500; proceeds for lost or destroyed exempt property; sewing machine.

Public Benefits

Unemployment compensation, workers' compensation except as to child support.

Tools of the Trade

Tools of occupation to $1,200; uniforms, arms, and equipment of military; yoke of oxen or horse needed for farming or teaming.

Unpaid Wages

Earned but unpaid wages.

Appendix C

NEW JERSEY
(Federal exemptions ARE available)

Homestead
    None.

Insurance
    Annuity contract proceeds to $500 per month.
    Disability or death benefits for military member.
    Disability, death, medical, or hospital benefits for civil defense workers.
    Fraternal benefit society benefits.
    Group life or health policy or proceeds.
    Health or disability benefits.
    Life insurance proceeds if proceeds cannot be used to pay beneficiary's creditors.
    Life insurance proceeds or avails if debtor is not the insured.

Partnership Property
    Property of a business partnership.

Pensions
    Alcohol beverage control officers, city boards of health employees, civil defense workers, county employees, firefighters, police officers, traffic officers, judges, municipal employees, prison employees, public employees, school district employees, state police, street and water department employees, teachers; ERISA-qualified benefits.

Personal Property
    Goods and chattel, personal property, and stock or interest in corporations to $1,000 total; burial plots; clothing; furniture and household goods to $1,000.

Public Benefits
> Unemployment compensation, workers' compensation, others.

Unpaid Wages
> Ninety percent if earned but unpaid wages if income is under $7,500 (if income is in excess of $7,500, the judge decides the amount); wages of military personal.

Appendix C

NEW MEXICO
(Federal exemptions ARE available)

Homestead
Real property to $20,000 if married, widowed or support-
ing another; joint owners may double.

Insurance
Benevolent association benefits to $5,000.
Fraternal benefit society benefits.
Life, accident, health, or annuity benefits, withdrawal, or
cash value, if beneficiary is a New Mexican citizen.
Life insurance proceeds.

Miscellaneous
Ownership interest in an unincorporated association.

Partnership Property
Property of a business partnership.

Pensions
Pension or retirement benefits; public school employees.

Personal Property
Books, health equipment, and furniture; building materials
except from purchase money claims; clothing; cooperative
association share (minimum amount needed to be a member); jewelry to $2,500; materials, tools, and machinery to
dig, torpedo, drill, complete, operate, or repair oil line, gas
well, or pipeline except as to purchase money claims; motor
vehicle to $4,000; $500 in any personal property; $2,000 in
lieu of homestead.

Tools of the Trade
$1,500 in tools.

Unpaid Wages

Greater of 75 percent of earned but unpaid wages or forty times the minimum wage except as to child support obligations.

Appendix C

NEW YORK
(Federal exemptions CANNOT be used)

Alimony
Alimony and child support needed for support.

Homestead
Real property including cooperative, condominium, or mobile home to $10,000; proceeds from sale are exempt for one year; husband and wife may double.

Insurance
Annuity contract benefits, if purchased within six months of filing for bankruptcy and not tax-deferred to $5,000.
Disability or illness benefits to $400 per month.
Fraternal benefit society benefits.
Insurance proceeds for damaged exempt property.
Life insurance proceeds if proceeds cannot be used to pay beneficiary's creditors.
Life insurance proceeds or avails if beneficiary is not the insured.

Partnership Property
Property of a business partnership.

Pensions
ERISA-qualified benefits including Keoghs and IRAs needed for support; public retirement benefits, state employees, village police officers.

Personal Property
Bible, school books, books to $50, pictures, clothing, church pew or seat, stoves with fuel to last sixty days, sewing machine, domestic animal with food to last sixty days to $45, food to last sixty days, furniture, refrigerator, televi-

sion, radio, wedding ring, watch to $35, crockery, cooking utensils, and tableware, to $5,000 total; burial plot without structure to one-quarter acre; cash--the lesser of $2,500 or an amount that with annuity total $5,000 in lieu of homestead; health aids; lost earnings recoveries needed for support; motor vehicle to $2,400; personal injury recoveries to $7,500 (not including pain and suffering); security deposits to landlord, utility company; trust fund principal (90 percent of income); wrongful death recoveries for person you depended upon.

Public Benefits

Unemployment compensation, worker's compensations, others.

Tools of the Trade

Uniforms, medal, equipment, emblem, horse, arms, and sword of military member.

Unpaid Wages

Ninety percent of earnings from milk sales to milk dealers; 90 percent of earned but unpaid wages received within sixty days of the bankruptcy filing.

NORTH CAROLINA
(Federal exemptions CANNOT be used)

Homestead
Real or personal property, including a cooperative, used as a residence to $7,500; property held as tenancy by the entireties may be exempt against debts owed by only one spouse; up to $2,500 of unused portion of homestead may be applied to any property.

Insurance
Fraternal benefit society benefits.
Group life policy or proceeds.
Life insurance policy if beneficiary is insured's spouse or child;
Life insurance proceeds or avails.

Partnership Property
Property of a business partnership.

Pensions
Firefighters and rescue squad workers; law enforcement officers; legislators; municipal, city, and county employees; teachers; and state employees.

Personal Property
Animals, crops, musical instrument, books, clothing, appliances, household goods and furnishings to $2,500 total; burial plot to $7,500 in lieu of homestead; health aids; motor vehicle to $1,000 except if purchased within ninety days of filing; personal injury recoveries for person you depended upon subject to child support; wrongful death recoveries for person you depended upon subject to child support; $2,500 of any property less any amount claimed for homestead or burial exemption.

Public Benefits
> Unemployment compensation subject to debts for necessities and child support, workers' compensation, others.

Tools of the Trade
> Implements, books, and tools of trade to $500.
> Unpaid Wages
> Earned but unpaid wages received sixty days before filing for bankruptcy needed for support.

NORTH DAKOTA
(Federal exemptions ARE available)

Homestead
Real property, house trailer, or mobile home to $80,000.

Insurance

Fraternal benefit society benefits.

Life insurance proceeds payable to deceased's estate, not to specific beneficiary.

Life insurance surrender value to $100,000 per policy if beneficiary is insured's relative and owned over one year before the bankruptcy filing.

Partnership Property
Property of a business partnership.

Pensions
Annuities, pensions, IRAs, Keoghs, simplified employee plans, and other ERISA-qualified benefits to $100,000 per plan with a limit of $200,000 for all pensions and life insurance policies; disabled veterans' benefits; public employees; state employees.

Personal Property
All debtors may exempt Bible, books to $100, pictures; clothing; burial plots, church pew; cash to $7,500 in lieu of homestead; crops or grain raised on debtor's tract to 160 acres on one tract; food and fuel to last one year; motor vehicle to $1,200; personal injury recoveries to $7,500 (not including pain and suffering); wrongful death recoveries to $7,500.

Head of household not claiming crops or grain may claim
$5,000 of any personal property or books and musical in-
struments to $1,500; furniture, including bedsteads and
bedding to $1,000; library and tools of professional to
$1,000; livestock and farm implements to $4,500; tools of
mechanics and stock in trade to $1,000.

Non-head of household not claiming crops or grain may
claim $2,500 of any personal property.

Public Benefits

Unemployment compensation except for necessities and if
funds are not commingled, workers' compensation except
for child support.

Unpaid Wages

Minimum of 75 percent of earned but unpaid wages.

Appendix C

OHIO
(Federal exemptions CANNOT be used)

Alimony
Alimony and child support needed for support.

Homestead
Real or personal property used as a residence to $5,000; property held by tenancy by the entireties may be exempt against debts owed by only one spouse.

Insurance
Benevolent society benefits to $5,000.
Disability benefits to $600 per month.
Fraternal benefit society benefits.
Group life insurance policy or proceeds.
Life, endowment, or annuity contract avails for your spouse, child, or dependent.
Life insurance proceeds for a spouse.
Life insurance proceeds if proceeds cannot be used to pay beneficiary's creditors.

Partnership Property
Property of a business partnership.

Pensions
ERISA-qualified benefits, IRAs, Keoghs needed for support; firefighters, police officers pensions and death benefits, public employees, public school employees, state highway patrol employees, volunteer firefighters' dependents.

Personal Property
Animals, crops, books, musical instruments, jewelry, appliances, household goods, furnishings, hunting and fishing equipment, and firearms to $200 per item, $1,500 total

($2,000 if no homestead is claimed); beds, bedding, and clothing to $200 per item; burial plot; cash, money due within ninety days, bank and security deposits, and tax refund to $400 total; cooking unit and refrigerator to $300 each; health aids; lost future earnings needed for support; motor vehicle to $2,000; personal injury recoveries to $5,000 (not including pain and suffering); wrongful death recoveries for person debtor depended upon; $400 in any property.

Public benefits
Unemployment compensation, workers' compensation, others.

Tools of the Trade
Implements, books, and tools of the trade to $750.

Unpaid Wages
Greater of thirty times minimum wage or 75 percent of disposable earnings.

OKLAHOMA

(Federal exemptions CANNOT be used)

Alimony

> Alimony and child support to the extent reasonably necessary for support.

Homestead

> Real property or manufactured home to unlimited value; property cannot exceed one-quarter acre; if property exceeds one-quarter acre, exemption is $5,000 for one acre in city, town, or village or 160 acres elsewhere; homestead need not be occupied so long as another is not acquired.

Insurance

> Assessment or mutual benefits.
> Fraternal benefit society benefits.
> Funeral benefits prepaid and place in trust.
> Group life policy or proceeds if you are not the insured.
> Life insurance policy or proceeds if you are not the insured.
> Limited stock insurance benefits.
> Money or benefits from any life, health, or accident insurance policy issued by a mutual benefit association or under any plan or program of annuities and benefits.

Partnership Property

> Property of a business partnership.

Pensions

> County employees, disabled veterans, firefighters, law enforcement employees, police officers, public employees, teachers; ERISA-qualified benefits and tax-exempt benefits.

Personal Property

Books, portraits, pictures, and gun; two bridles and two saddles; burial plots and funds in trust for prepaid funeral benefits; 100 chickens, ten hogs, two horses, five cows, and calves under six months, twenty sheep; forage for livestock to last one year; clothing to $4,000; furniture; health aids; motor vehicle to $3,000; personal injury, wrongful death, and workers' compensation recoveries to $50,000 (cannot include punitive or exemplary damages).

Public Benefits

Unemployment compensation, workers' compensation except for necessities and child support, others.

Tools of the Trade

Husbandry implements to farm homestead, tools, books, and apparatus to $5,000 total.

Unpaid Wages

Seventy-five percent of wages earned in ninety days before the bankruptcy filing.

OREGON
(Federal exemptions CANNOT be used)

Alimony
> Alimony and child support needed for support.

Homestead
> Real property, mobile home, or house boat to $15,000 ($20,000 for joint owners); $13,000 for mobile home if land is not owned ($18,000 for joint owners; property cannot exceed one lot in town or city or 160 acres elsewhere; sale proceeds are exempt for one year from sale if you intend to purchase another home; homestead must be occupied or intended to be occupied at the time of filing.

Insurance
> Annuity contract benefits to $250 per month.
> Fraternal benefit society benefits.
> Group life policy or proceeds.
> Health or disability proceeds or avails.
> Life insurance proceeds if proceeds cannot be used to pay beneficiary's creditors.
> Life insurance proceeds or cash value if you are not the insured.

Miscellaneous
> Liquor license.

Partnership Property
> Property of a business partnership.

Pensions
> IRAs and tax-qualified employee pension plans except as to child support obligations; government (federal, state, local)

employees, public officers and employees, school district employees.

Personal Property

Bank deposits to $7,500, cash from sale of exempt property; books, pictures, and musical instruments to $300 (husband and wife may double); burial plot; clothing, jewelry, and other personal items to $900 total (husband and wife may double); domestic animals, poultry with food to last sixty days to $1,000; food and fuel to last sixty days if debtor is householder; furniture, household items, utensils, radios, and televisions to $1,450 total; health aids; lost-earnings payments for debtor or someone debtor depended upon to the extent needed; motor vehicle to $1,200 (husband and wife may double); personal injury recoveries to $7,500, not including pain and suffering (husband and wife may double); pistol, rifle, or shotgun if owned by someone over sixteen; $400 of any personal property (husband and wife may double so long as existing exemption is not increased).

Public Benefits

Unemployment compensation, workers' compensation, others.

Tools of the Trade

Tools, library, team with food to last sixty days to $750 (husband and wife may double).

Unpaid Wages

Minimum of 75 percent of earned but unpaid wages and wages withheld in employees bond savings account.

PENNSYLVANIA
(Federal exemptions ARE available)

Homestead

    None except that property held by tenant by the entirety may be exempt against debtors owed by only one spouse.

Insurance

    Accident or disability benefits.

    Fraternal benefit society benefits.

    Group life policy or proceeds.

    Life insurance annuity contract payments, cash value, or proceeds to $100 per month.

    Life insurance annuity policy, cash value, or proceeds if beneficiary is insured's dependent, child or spouse.

    Life insurance proceeds if proceeds cannot be used to pay beneficiary's creditors.

    No-fault automobile insurance proceeds.

Partnership Property

    Property of a business partnership.

Pensions

    City employees, county employees, municipal employees, police officers, public school employees, state employees; self-employment benefits; employer-sponsored pensions or annuities if contractually nonassignable except as to amounts contributed within one year of bankruptcy and in excess of $15,000 within one year.

Personal Property

    Bibles, school books, sewing machine, clothing; tangible personal property at an international exhibit sponsored by the United States government; uniforms and accoutrements; $300 of any property.

Public Benefits
> Unemployment compensation as long as payments are not commingled and except to the extent of necessities and child support, workers' compensation, others.

Unpaid Wages
> Earned but unpaid wages.

RHODE ISLAND
(Federal exemptions ARE available)

Homestead
>None.

Insurance
>Accident or sickness proceeds, avails or benefits.
>Fraternal benefit society benefits.
>Life insurance proceeds if proceeds cannot be used to pay beneficiary's creditors.
>Life insurance proceeds or avails if beneficiary is not the insured.
>Temporary disability insurance.

Miscellaneous
>Earnings of minor children.

Partnership Property
>Property of a business partnership.

Pensions
>ERISA-qualified benefits including IRAs except if subject to divorce judgment or separate maintenance or child support; firefighters, police officers, private employees, state and municipal employees.

Personal Property
>Beds, bedding, furniture, and family stores of a housekeeper to $1,000 total; Bibles and books to $300; burial plot; clothing needed; consumer cooperative association holdings to $50; debt secured by promissory note or bill of exchange.

Public Benefits
Unemployment compensation as long as funds are not commingled, workers' compensation, others.

Tools of the Trade
Library of a professional in practice; working tools to $500.

Unpaid Wages
Earned but unpaid wages to $50; earned but unpaid wages due to military member on active duty; earned but unpaid wages due seaman; earned but unpaid wages if welfare was received within the year preceding the bankruptcy filing; wages of spouse; wages paid by charitable organizations to the poor.

Appendix C

SOUTH CAROLINA
(Federal exemptions ARE available)

Alimony
> Alimony and child support.

Homestead
> Real property including a cooperative to $5,000; joint owners may double.

Insurance
> Disability or illness benefits.
> Fraternal benefit society benefits.
> Life insurance avails from policy for person you depended upon to $4,000.
> Life insurance proceeds for spouse or child to $25,000.
> Life insurance proceeds from policy for person you depended on as needed for support.
> Life insurance proceeds if proceeds cannot be used to pay beneficiary's creditors.
> Unmatured life insurance contract.

Partnership Property
> Property of a business partnership.

Pensions
> ERISA-qualified benefits; firefighters, general assembly members, judges, solicitors, police officers, public employees.

Personal Property
> Animal, crops, appliances, books, clothing, household goods, furnishings, musical instruments to $2,500 total; burial lot to $5,000 in lieu of homestead; cash and other liquid assets to $1,000 in lieu of burial or homestead ex-

emption; health aids; jewelry to $500; motor vehicle to $1,200; personal injury recoveries; wrongful death recoveries.

Public Benefits
Unemployment compensation, workers' compensation, others.

Tools of the Trade
Implements, books and tools of trade to $750.
Unpaid Wages
All wages.

SOUTH DAKOTA
(Federal exemptions CANNOT be used)

Homestead
> Real property or mobile home larger than 240 square feet at its base and registered in state at least six months before filing to an unlimited value; property cannot exceed one acre in town or 160 acres elsewhere; sale proceeds to $30,000 are exempt for one year after sale unless you are over seventy, in which case the exemption amount is unlimited; spouse of child of a deceased owner may claim the homestead exemption; the acreage is limited if the homestead is mineral or mining land.

Insurance
> Annuity contract proceeds to $250 per month.
> Endowment, life insurance policy, proceeds or cash value to $20,000.
> Fraternal benefit society benefits.
> Health benefits to $20,000.
> Life insurance proceeds if proceeds cannot be used to pay beneficiary's creditors.
> Life insurance proceeds to $10,000 if beneficiary is surviving spouse or child.

Partnership Property
> Property of a business partnership.

Pensions
> City employees and public employees.

Personal Property
> All debtors may exempt Bible, books to $200, pictures, burial plots, church pew, food and fuel to last one year, and clothing.

Head of family may claim $4,000 of any personal property or books and musical instruments to $200; two cows, five swine, twenty-five sheep with lambs under six months, wool, cloth or yarn of sheep, food for all to last one year; farming machinery, utensils, tackle for teams, harrow, two plows, sleigh, wagon to $1,250 total; furniture, including bedsteads and bedding to $200; library and tools of professional to $300; tools of mechanic and stock in trade to $200; two yoke of oxen or span of horses or mules.
Non-head of family may claim $2,000 of any personal property.

Public Benefits
Unemployment compensation except as to necessities and child support, workers' compensation except as to support obligations.

Unpaid Wages
Earned wages owed sixty days before filing for bankruptcy, needed for support of family and 80 percent of disposable income unless garnisheed for support; wages of prisoners in work programs.

Appendix C

TENNESSEE
(Federal exemptions CANNOT be used)

Alimony
> Alimony owed for thirty days before filing for bankruptcy.

Homestead
> Five thousand dollars; $7,500 for joint owners; property held by tenants by the entirety may be exempt against debts owed by only one spouse; exemptions may be claimed for life estates and leases; spouse or child of deceased owner may claim the exemption.

Insurance
> Accident, health or disability benefits.
> Disability or illness benefits.
> Fraternal benefit society benefits.
> Homeowners' insurance proceeds to $5,000.
> Life insurance proceeds or cash values if beneficiary is debtor's dependent, child, or spouse.

Partnership Property
> Property of a business partnership.

Pensions
> ERISA-qualified benefits; public employees, state and local government employees; teachers.

Personal Property
> Bible, school books, pictures, portraits; burial plot to one acre; clothing and storage containers; health aids; lost earnings payments for you or a person you depended upon; personal injury recoveries to $7,500 (not including pain and suffering); wrongful death recoveries to $10,000 (claim for personal injury, wrongful death or crime victims' compen-

sation cannot exceed $15,000); $4,000 of any personal property.

Public Benefits

Unemployment compensations, workers' compensation, others.

Tools of the Trade

Implements, books, and tools of trade to $7,500.

Unpaid Wages

Minimum of 75 percent of earned but unpaid wages, plus $2.50 per week per child or thirty times federal minimum hourly wage amount.

Appendix C

TEXAS
(Federal exemptions ARE available)

Homestead

Unlimited; property cannot exceed one acre in town, village, or city or 100 acres elsewhere (200 acres for families); sale proceeds are exempt for six months after sale.

Insurance

Fraternal benefit society benefits.

Life, health, accident, or annuity benefits.

Life insurance present value if beneficiary is debtor or debtor's dependent.

Life insurance proceeds if proceeds cannot be used to pay beneficiary's creditors.

Retired public school employees group insurance.

Texas employee uniform group insurance.

Texas state college or university employee benefits.

Partnership Property

Property of a business partnership.

Pensions

ERISA-qualified government or church benefits including Keoghs and IRAs; retirement benefits including IRAs, Keoghs and simplified employee plans to the extent tax-deferred; county and district employees, firefighters, judges, law enforcement officers' survivors, municipal employees, police officers, state employees, teachers.

Personal Property

Athletic and sporting equipment, including bicycles; two firearms; home furnishings, including heirlooms; food; clothing; jewelry (not to exceed 25 percent of total exemption); one two-,three- or four-wheeled motor vehicle per

275

family member with a drivers' license; two horses, mules, or donkeys and a saddle, blanket, and bridle for each; twelve head of cattle, sixty head of other livestock, one hundred twenty fowl and pets to $30,000 total ($60,000 for head of family; burial plots; health aids.

Public Benefits
Unemployment compensation, workers' compensation, others.

Tools of the Trade
Farming or ranching vehicles and implements; tools, equipment, including boat and motor vehicles, books.

Unpaid Wages
Earned but unpaid wages; unpaid commissions to 75 percent.

276

Appendix C

UTAH
(Federal exemptions CANNOT be used)

Alimony
>Alimony needed for support.

Homestead
>Real property, mobile home, or water rights to $8,000; $2,000 added for spouse and $500 per dependent; homestead declaration must be filed before bankruptcy filing.

Insurance
>Disability, illness, medical, or hospital benefits.
>Fraternal benefit society benefits.
>Life insurance policy cash surrender value to $1,500.
>Life insurance proceeds if beneficiary is insured's spouse or dependent as needed for support.

Partnership Property
>Property of a business partnership.

Pensions
>ERISA-qualified benefits; public employees; other pensions needed for support.

Personal Property
>Animals, books and musical instruments to $500 total; artwork depicting or done by family member; bed, bedding, carpets, washer and dryer; burial plot; clothing except for furs and jewelry; food to last three months; furnishings and appliances to $500; health aids as needed; heirlooms or other sentimental items to $500; personal injury recoveries for you or a dependent; refrigerator, freezer, stove, and sewing machine; wrongful death recoveries for person you depended upon.

Public Benefits
> Unemployment compensation except as to necessities, workers' compensation, others.

Tools of the Trade
> Implements, books, and tools of the trade to $1,500; military property of national guard member; motor vehicle to $1,500.

Unpaid Wages
> Seventy-five percent of wages or thirty times the federal minimum wage.

Appendix C

VERMONT
(Federal exemptions ARE available)

Alimony
> Alimony and child support needed for support.

Homestead
> Real property or mobile home to $30,000; rents, issues, profits and outbuildings may be claimed; property held by tenants by the entirety may be exempt against debts owed by only one spouse; spouse of deceased owner may claim homestead exemption.

Insurance
> Annuity contract benefits to $300 per month.
> Disability or illness benefits needed for support.
> Fraternal benefit society benefits.
> Group life or health benefits.
> Health benefits to $200 per month.
> Life insurance proceeds if beneficiary is not the insured.
> Life insurance proceeds for person you depended upon.
> Life insurance proceeds if proceeds cannot be used to pay beneficiary's creditors.
> Unmatured life insurance contract other than credit.

Partnership Property
> Property of a business partnership.

Pensions
> Self-directed accounts (IRAs, Keoghs) to $10,000; municipal employees, state employees, teachers, other pensions.

Personal Property
> Appliances, furnishings, goods, clothing books, crops, animals, musical instruments to $2,500 total; cow, two goats,

ten sheep, ten chickens, three swarms of bees and their honey; feed to last one winter; ten cords of firewood; five tons of coal or 500 gallons of oil; 500 gallons of bottled gas; growing crops to $5,000; two harnesses, two halters, two chains, plow and ox yoke, yoke of oxen or steers, and two horses; jewelry to $500; wedding ring unlimited; motor vehicles to $2,500; bank deposits to $700; personal injury recoveries for person you depended upon; stove, heating unit, refrigerator, freezer, water heater, sewing machines; lost future earnings for you or person you depended on; health aids; wrongful death recoveries for person you depended upon; $7,000 of any property, less any amount of appliances, etc., growing crops, jewelry, motor vehicle and tools of trade; $400 of any property.

Public Benefits
Unemployment compensation, workers' compensation, others.

Tools of the Trade
Books and tools of trade to $5,000.

Unpaid Wages
Minimum of 75 percent of earned but unpaid wages; wages if received during two months before filing.

Appendix C

VIRGINIA
(Federal exemptions CANNOT be used)

Homestead

 Property to $5,000, plus $500 for each dependent; rents
 and profits may also be claimed; property held as tenancy by
 the entirety may be exempt against debts owed by only one
 spouse; homestead declaration must be filed prior to bankruptcy filing; unused portion of homestead may be applied
 to any personal property.

Insurance

 Accident or sickness benefits.
 Burial society benefits.
 Cooperative life insurance benefits.
 Fraternal benefit society benefits.
 Group life or accident insurance for government officials.
 Group life insurance policy or proceeds.
 Industrial sick benefits.
 Life insurance cash values to $10,000.
 Life insurance proceeds or avails if beneficiary is not the in-
 sured.

Partnership Property
 Property of a business partnership

Pensions
 ERISA-qualified benefits to $17,500 per year; county em-
 ployees, judges, state employees.

Personal Property
 For householders, Bible, family portraits, and heirlooms to
 $5,000 total; burial plot; clothing to $1,000; health aids;
 household furnishings to $5,000 plus $500 for each dependent; pets; motor vehicle to $2,000; personal injury causes

of action; personal injury recoveries; wedding and engagement rings; military equipment; $2,000 in any property for disabled veterans.

Public Benefits

Unemployment compensation, workers' compensation, others.

Tools of the Trade

Horses, mules (pair) with gear, wagon or cart tractor to $3,000, two plows, drag, harvest cradle, pitchfork, rake, two iron wedges, fertilizer to $1,000 for householder; tools, books and instruments of trade, including motor vehicles to $10,000 needed for occupation or education of householder; uniforms, arms, and equipment of military member.

Unpaid Wages

Greater of 75 percent of earned but unpaid wages or thirty times the federal minimum wage amount.

Appendix C

WASHINGTON
(Federal exemptions ARE available)

Homestead
>   Real property or mobile home to $30,000; homestead dec-
>   laration must be recorded prior to sale if the property is un-
>   improved or unoccupied.

Insurance
>   Annuity contract proceeds to $250 per month.
>   Disability proceeds, avails or benefits.
>   Fire insurance proceeds for destroyed exemption.
>   Fraternal benefit society benefits.
>   Group life insurance policy or proceeds.
>   Life insurance proceeds or avails if beneficiary is not the in-
>   sured.

Partnership Property
>   Property of a business partnership.

Pensions
>   Except as to claims for child support: ERISA-qualified
>   benefits, including IRAs; city employees, public employees,
>   state patrol officers, volunteer firefighters.

Personal Property
>   Appliances, furniture, household goods, home and yard
>   equipment to $2,775 total; books to $1,500; burial plots
>   sold by nonprofit cemetery association; clothing except that
>   furs, jewelry and ornaments cannot exceed $1,000; keep-
>   sakes and pictures; motor vehicle to $2,500; $1,000 in any
>   personal property (no more than $100 in cash, bank depos-
>   its, bonds, stocks and securities).

Public Benefits
> Unemployment compensation, others.

Tools of the Trade
> Farm trucks, stock, tools, seed, equipment, and supplies of farmer to $5,000 total; library, office furniture, office equipment, and supplies of physician, surgeon, attorney, clergy, or other professional to $5,000 total; tools and materials used in another's trade to $5,000.

Unpaid Wages
> Greater of 75 percent of earned but unpaid wages or thirty times the federal minimum wage amount of disposable income.

WEST VIRGINIA
(Federal exemptions CANNOT be used)

Alimony
> Alimony and child support as needed for support.

Homestead
> Real or personal property used as a residence to $7,500; unused portion of homestead may be applied to any property.

Insurance
> Fraternal benefit society benefits.
> Group life insurance policy or proceeds.
> Health or disability benefits.
> Life insurance avails to $4,000 from policy of person you depended upon.
> Life insurance proceeds unless you are both policy owner and beneficiary.
> Life insurance proceeds or cash value if beneficiary is married woman.
> Unmatured life insurance contract, except credit life insurance contract.

Partnership Property
> Property of a business partnership.

Pensions
> ERISA-qualified benefits needed for support; public employees, teachers.

Personal Property
> Animals, crops, clothing, appliances, books, household goods, furnishings, musical instruments to $200 per item, $1,000 total; burial plot to $7,500 in lieu of homestead;

health aids; jewelry to $500; lost earnings payments needed for support; motor vehicle to $1,200; personal injury recoveries to $7,500 (not including pain and suffering); wrongful death recoveries needed for support from person you depended upon; $400 or any property; unused portion of homestead or burial exemption.

Public Benefits

Unemployment compensation, workers' compensation, others.

Tools of the Trade

Implements, books, and tools of the trade to $750.

Unpaid Wages

Eighty percent of earned but unpaid wages or thirty times the federal minimum hourly wage per week.

WISCONSIN
(Federal exemptions ARE available)

Alimony
> Alimony and child support needed for support.

Homestead
> Forty thousand dollars; sale proceeds are exempt for two years from sale if you plan to purchase another home; homestead must be occupied or intended to be occupied at the time of filing; husband and wife may not double.

Insurance
> Federal disability insurance benefits.
>
> Fire and casualty insurance and proceeds for destroyed exempt property for two years after receipt.
>
> Fraternal benefit society benefits.
>
> Health, accident, or disability benefits to $150 per month.
>
> Life insurance policy or proceeds to $5,000 if beneficiary is a married woman.
>
> Life insurance proceeds cannot be used to pay beneficiary's creditors.
>
> Life insurance proceeds if beneficiary is debtor's dependent or person on whom debtor depended.
>
> Unmatured life insurance contract to $4,000.

Partnership Property
> Property of a business partnership.

Pensions
> Certain municipal employees, firefighters, police officers in cities with populations in excess of 100,000, military pensions, private or public retirement benefits, public employees.

Personal Property

Burial provision; deposit accounts to $1,000; household goods and furnishings, clothing, keepsakes, jewelry, appliances, books, musical instruments, firearms, sporting goods, animals, and other tangible property held for personal, family or household use to $5,000 total; lost-future-earnings recoveries needed for support; motor vehicle to $1,200; personal injury recoveries to $25,000; tenant's lease or stock interest in housing cooperative; wages used to purchase savings bonds; wrongful death recoveries needed for support.

Public Benefits

Unemployment compensation except as to child support obligations, workers' compensation, others.

Tools of the Trade

Equipment, inventory, farm products, books, and tools of trade to $7,500 total.

Unpaid Wages

Seventy-five percent of earned but unpaid wages but not less than thirty times the federal minimum wage amount.

Appendix C

WYOMING
(Federal exemptions CANNOT be used)

Homestead
> Real property to $10,000 or house trailer to $6,000; property held as tenancy by the entirety may be exempt against debts owed by only one spouse; joint owners may double; homestead must be occupied at the time of the bankruptcy filing; spouse or child of deceased owner may claim homestead exemption.

Insurance
> Annuity contract proceeds to $350 per month.
> Disability benefits if proceeds cannot be used to pay beneficiary's creditors.
> Fraternal benefit society benefits.
> Group life or disability policy or proceeds.
> Life insurance proceeds if beneficiary is not the insured.

Miscellaneous
> Liquor licenses and malt beverage permits.

Partnership Property
> Property of a business partnership.

Pension
> Criminal investigators, highway officers, firefighters, police officers (only payments being received), game and fish wardens, public employees, public and private employers' pensions when plan provides that benefits are not assignable.

Personal Property
> Bedding, furniture, household articles, and food to $2,000 per person in the home except as to purchase money debts; Bible, school books and pictures, burial plot, motor vehicle

to $2,000; clothing and wedding rings to $1,000; prepaid funeral contracts.

Public Benefits

Unemployment compensation, except as to claims for necessities during unemployment, workers' compensation, except as to claims for child support, others.

Tools of the Trade

Library and implements of professional to $2,000 or tools, motor vehicle, implements, team, and stock in trade to $2,000.

Unpaid Wages

Earning of national guard members; 75 percent of weekly disposable income or thirty times the federal minimum wage whichever is greater; wages of inmates on work release.

Appendix D

Glossary

This glossary explains the technical words found in the book. The word is explained the first time it is used, but this listing will provide a handy reference. When a word is italicized, it means that word can be found elsewhere in the glossary if you do not understand it.

Abandonment: the process by which the *trustee* releases property from the *estate*. It is generally done when the amount of *secured claims* against the property exceeds the value of the property. Once property has been abandoned, it can be dealt with as if a bankruptcy petition had not been filed.

Administrative claim: a claim arising while a Chapter 7 or 13 case is pending. Administrative claims generally are entitled to payment before any prepetition claims are paid. Trustees' fees are administrative claims.

Adversary proceeding: a special procedure brought within a pending bankruptcy case. It is generally used to assert that a debt is nondischargeable or that a debtor is not entitled to a discharge (see part 9) or to recover fraudulent transfers and other property of the estate (see part 12).

Alleged debtor: when creditors file an *involuntary petition* against an individual, that person is called the alleged debtor until the court determines that the case should proceed. That individual then becomes a *debtor*.

Automatic stay: an injunction that issues automatically upon the filing of petitions under the *Bankruptcy Code*. The automatic stay protects *debtors* from debt-enforcement actions by creditors. See part 6. In *Chapter 13* proceedings it also offers some protection to *co-debtors* (guarantors and co-makers).

Bankrupt: see *Debtor*.

Bankruptcy Code: laws of the United States designed to give debtors a fresh start financially. The current bankruptcy laws are contained in the *Bankruptcy Code*, which is title 11 of the United States Code. A particular section of the Bankruptcy Code, such as section 341, is designated as 11 U.S.C. § 341.

Bankruptcy Court: a part of the *United States District Court* designated to hear bankruptcy cases and matters arising in them.

Bankruptcy crimes: conduct proscribed by federal statutes that make certain conduct in connection with a bankruptcy a criminal offense. See part 16.

Bankruptcy Judge: a judge appointed by the federal circuit court of appeals to preside in bankruptcy matters only. Bankruptcy Judges are usually appointed for a term of fourteen years. There may be one or more judges in a district.

Bankruptcy laws: see *Bankruptcy Code*.

Best interests of creditors: one of the tests for approval of a Chapter 13 plan. See part 7.

Borrower: a person who takes out a loan. See *Guarantor.*

Chapter 7: the portion of the *Bankruptcy Code* that deals with liquidations. Sometimes called "straight bankruptcy." See part 6.

Chapter 11: the portion of the *Bankruptcy Code* that deals with reorganizations. It is generally used only by businesses, or persons with significant unincorporated business interests, and is not discussed in this book.

Chapter 12: the portion of the *Bankruptcy Code* that deals with reorganization by family farmers. Although this book does not discuss Chapter 12, the rules for qualifying under it are summarized at the end of part 5.

Chapter 13: the portion of the *Bankruptcy Code* that deals with debt adjustment for individuals with regular incomes. Arrangements under this chapter were formerly called "wage-earner plans." See parts 7 and 8.

Chapter 13 Plan: a plan filed by the *debtor* under *Chapter 13* to pay debts over a period of three to five years. See part 8.

Chapter 13 trustee: a *trustee in bankruptcy* who specializes in cases under *Chapter 13.* One or just a few Chapter 13 trustees generally handle all of the Chapter 13 cases in a particular court.

Co-debtor: A guaranty (or guarantee) is a promise to pay the debt of someone else. It is generally represented

by a signature of the guarantor on a special form provided by a lender. A co-maker generally signs on the
same piece of paper as the *borrower*. With some very
technical differences, which generally do not make any
practical difference, a co-maker is responsible for the
debts of the other person in the same way as a guarantor. A guarantor or co-maker is also sometimes called
a co-debtor. The responsibility of such parties is covered in part 15.

Co-maker: see *Co-debtor*.

Confirmation: process by which Bankruptcy Court approves a *Chapter 13* plan. See part 7.

Consensual liens: see *Lien*.

Consumer debt: a debt incurred by an individual primarily for a personal, family, or household purpose.

Conversion: the process whereby a pending bankruptcy
case is moved from (most commonly) Chapter 13 to
Chapter 7, or between other chapters. It can be done
by the court, on a motion by a creditor, or by the
debtor.

Creditor: the person or business to whom money or property is owed. Certain creditors, such as taxing authorities, have priority in payment. Other creditors are
general creditors, who have a claim for money, but no
collateral or security for payment. Secured creditors
have a claim against a specific asset or group of assets to
secure payment of the amount due.

Debtor: usually the person who files a *petition for relief.* In the case of an *involuntary petition,* the petition is filed by creditors and, until the court determines that the petition is proper, the person against whom it is filed is called the *alleged debtor.* When a husband and wife file a joint petition, the first named is called the debtor and sometimes the other is called spouse; collectively they are the "debtors." Under earlier laws, the person now called the debtor was called the "bankrupt."

Discharge: a court order that wipes out debts formerly owed. See part 9 for information about the types of debts that may not be dischargeable. The discharge is embodied in an order to creditors holding discharged debts to refrain from taking any action to collect their debts. If a creditor should do so, it is in contempt of the Bankruptcy Court.

Dischargeability: a determination of whether a claim will be discharged in bankruptcy is called a determination of dischargeability. See part 9.

Dismissal: a bankruptcy case can be dismissed for a variety of reasons described in the book. Most usual is a debtor's failure to cooperate or file proper documents or a determination by the Bankruptcy Court that the petition was filed in bad faith. Dismissal terminates the case without a discharge. It may also prohibit the filing of a new petition for a period of time.

Estate: the property of the *debtor* being administered by the trustee under the Bankruptcy Code.

Execution: see *Judgment.*

Executory contract: a contract that has not been completely performed by the parties at the time of the bankruptcy filing.

Exemptions: certain types of assets and certain amounts of money that the debtor may claim and that do not become *property of the estate*. See part 11.

Expenses of administration: the costs of running a bankruptcy *estate*. They include fees due to the *Bankruptcy Court*, fees due to the *United States Trustee* (in certain cases), attorneys' fees, and trustees' fees. Expenses of administration are paid before any unsecured *claims*.

Fair market value: the theoretical price that a willing buyer would pay to a willing seller for something.

Family farmer: a person, married couple, or qualified partnership or corporation eligible for relief under Chapter 12 of the Bankruptcy Code. Chapter 12 is not covered in detail in this book, but eligibility requirements are set out in part 5.

Filing fee: the fee charged by the court for the filing of a petition or a complaint to determine the dischargeability of a debt or the denial of a discharge. At present the filing fee under Chapters 7 and 13 and the fee for filing a complaint are $120. An administrative fee of $30 was added in December 1992.

First meeting of creditors: see *Section 341 meeting*.

Forced sale: a sale by auction or otherwise to collect a debt. It generally will not bring the *fair market value* of the property, but a lesser amount, often called liquidation value.

Fraudulent conveyance: see *Fraudulent transfer.*

Fraudulent transfer: also called a "fraudulent conveyance." A transfer by a *debtor,* before bankruptcy, of assets for less than they were worth or in fraud of creditors. See part 12.

General creditor: see *Creditor.*

Guarantor: a person who signs a guaranty. See *Co-debtor.*

Guaranty (or guarantee): see *Co-debtor.*

Hardship discharge, Chapter 13: see part 7.

Injunction: a court order directed to a person or organization either forbidding the performance of an act and directing an act to be performed. Injunctions are sometimes coupled with *sanctions.*

Insiders: persons or organizations having certain types of close familial or financial relationships to a debtor.

Insolvency: for bankruptcy purposes, having debts exceeding the value of one's assets.

Intangible personal property: see *Personal property.*

Involuntary petition: a *petition* that is filed against someone (called the *alleged debtor*) by creditors. See part 14.

Judgment: a court order indicating that a person owes money or obligations to another. In many states, a judgment becomes a *lien* upon the property of the defendant as soon as it is entered. In others, the plaintiff must obtain an additional court order, called an execution, and file it before the lien arises.

Judicial lien: see *Lien.*

Lien: an interest in property held by a creditor to secure payment of money due. Voluntary or consensual liens are those freely given by a person, such as a mortgage to buy a house or a *security interest* in a car to finance its purchase. See Security interest. Judgment liens (also called judicial liens) are involuntary in that they arise from court action against the debtor, and are often called judgments, executions, attachments, or garnishments. Judgment liens are sometimes treated in special ways under the Bankruptcy Code. See part 13. See also *Tax liens.*

Liquidation value: see *Forced sale.*

Motion for relief from stay: see *Relief from stay.*

Net worth: a comparison of assets and liabilities. If assets are greater than liabilities, then net worth is positive. If the facts are the other way around, negative net worth is the result.

Nonpossessory non-purchase-money security interest: see *Security interest.*

Notice and hearing: under the *Bankruptcy Code,* "notice and hearing" means that notice of a proposed action must be given, but a hearing or trial may not be held if there is no *objection* to the proposal.

Objection: when someone objects to action proposed to be taken by a debtor, trustee, or creditor, an objection to that action is filed in writing with the Bankruptcy Court. The court will probably schedule a hearing on the objection.

Official Forms: a set of forms required to be used for filings in the Bankruptcy Court. The more important ones are reproduced in this book. Computer versions are authorized and are used by many attorneys.

Order for relief: an order of the Bankruptcy Court enjoining further creditor action to collect. It is entered automatically upon the filing of the bankruptcy petition in a voluntary case.

Personal property: all property other than *real property*. Tangible personal property is property you can touch, such as furniture or a car. Stocks and bank accounts are intangible personal property, because, even though they are represented by pieces of paper (stock certificates or bankbooks), the interests that they represent cannot be touched.

Petition; petition for relief: the first piece of paper filed in a bankruptcy case. It asks the court to give the relief sought, usually discharge of debts.

Postpetition: see *Prepetition.*

Preferences; preferential transfers: a transfer by an insolvent person to or for the benefit of a creditor made within the preference period on account of a debt owed before the transfer was made that gives the creditor more than it would have received in the bankruptcy if the transfer hadn't been made. See part 12.

Prepetition: things that happened before the original *petition* was filed in the case. Most postpetition events do not affect a Chapter 7 filing; some may affect proceedings under Chapter 13.

Priority claims: claims against a debtor that are entitled to payment before amounts due to other *creditors*. The most common examples are tax claims.

Property of the estate: that portion of the debtor's assets that comes under the control of the bankruptcy trustee. It is usually all of the debtor's assets less exempt assets. See part 11.

Purchase money security interest: see *Security interest.*

Reaffirmation: a method of keeping property by agreeing to continue making the scheduled payments. See part 13.

Real property: includes the usual kinds of ownership of real estate, and also covers condominiums, cooperative apartments, burial plots, and most time-share units. For bankruptcy schedule purposes, the interest of a tenant under a lease or rental is not considered real property.

Relief from stay, motion for: a secured *creditor*, such as the holder of a mortgage or another lender with security, is prohibited by the *automatic stay* from enforcing the mortgage or other *security interest*. If the creditor wishes to go against the property, it must ask the

Bankruptcy Court for permission to do so. The form of the request is a "motion for relief from stay." See part 13.

Revocation of discharge: if a *creditor,* the *United States Trustee,* or another interested party learns that a *discharge* has been obtained by fraud, that party may ask the Bankruptcy Court to revoke the discharge.

Rule 2004 examination: a creditor may obtain permission of the Bankruptcy Court, under rule 2004 of the Federal Rules of Bankruptcy Procedure, to have the debtor or other persons questioned under oath about the debtor's affairs.

Sanctions: penalties imposed by the Bankruptcy Court for violation of law or its orders. Sanctions are generally the issuance of an *injunction,* imposition of monetary penalties against the offender and sometimes the attorneys involved (commonly called "fines," but they really are something else), or dismissal of an action or a claim.

Schedules: the parts of the *Official Forms* that outline debts, assets, and exemptions.

Section 341 meeting: a meeting called by the Bankruptcy Court at which the debtor will be required to answer questions under oath asked by the *trustee* and creditors. It is also known as the "first meeting of creditors." See part 6.

Secured creditor: see *Creditor.*

Security interest: a voluntary interest that is given to a creditor to secure payment of either (1) the purchase price of property or (2) a loan secured by that property. The first type is called a purchase money security interest. In the usual case, the second kind is a non-possessory non-purchase-money security interest. They are treated differently for some purposes under the Bankruptcy Code. See part 13.

Spouse: see *Debtor.*

Statement of affairs: one of the *Official Forms.* It gives information about the debtor and things that the debtor has and has done.

Statement of intention: a statement filed by a debtor who wishes to surrender or keep certain types of consumer goods. See part 13.

Tangible personal property: see *Personal property.*

Tax lien: a lien that automatically arises on property on which property taxes are due. Real estate taxes always create a tax lien on the real estate. In some states, the assessment of personal property taxes also creates tax liens.

Trustee; trustee in bankruptcy: a court officer appointed by the *United States Trustee* (in most courts) to administer the *property of the estate.* The trustee is usually selected from a panel of trustees who handle many cases.

United States district court: the trial court in the federal system of courts. The *Bankruptcy Court* is technically part of the United States district court. See part 2.

United States Trustee: in most states, an official of the United States Department of Justice who appoints trustees and creditors' committees and exercises general oversight of bankruptcy cases.

Voluntary liens: see *Lien.*

Wage-earner plans: see *Chapter 13.*

Index

A

D

F

H

Hardship discharge in Chapter 13
    defined . . . 299
    generally . . . 58, 60-61
Hardship test for student loans . . . 82
Hawaii
    federal exemption . . . 93, 185
    state exemptions . . . 211-12
Health aids . . . 111
Health Education Assistance Loans . . . 82
Hearing on
    confirmation of Chapter 13 plan . . . 13, 45
    dischargeability . . . 12
Home mortgages . . . 67-69
Homestead exemption
    federal . . . 186
    state . . . *see* individual states
House . . . *see* Residence
Household furnishings and goods . . . 93, 36, 110
How bankruptcy works . . . 2, 5-13
Hypothetical Chapter 7 sale in Chapter 13 . . . 47-48

I

Idaho exemptions . . . 92, 213-14
Illinois exemptions . . . 92, 215-16
Implements . . . 111
Importance of
    automatic stay . . . 32-33
    avoiding liens . . . 94

Intentions
    filing statement of ... 12
    regarding consumer products subject to liens stated ... 36
Involuntary petitions
    defined ... 299
    filed by creditors ... 27-28
    generally ... 126-27
Iowa exemptions ... 92, 219-20
IRAs ... *see* Individual retirement accounts

J

Jewelry ... 94, 110
Joint petitions ... 26, 28
Judgments
    defined ... 300
    generally ... 105-06
Judicial liens
    avoiding ... 21
    defined ... 300

K

Kansas exemptions ... 92, 221-22
Keeping property after bankruptcy ... 105-12
Kentucky exemptions ... 92, 223-24
Knowingly concealing property of estate ... 133

Index

L

N

P

R

Virginia exemptions . . . 93, 281–82
Voluntary
    dismissals . . . 26
    liens, defined . . . 305
    nature of Chapter 13 . . . 42
    petitions . . . *see* Filing

W

Wage-earner plans
    defined . . . 305
    generally . . . 41
Wages, unpaid . . . 39
War-risk hazards . . . 92
Washington
    federal exemption . . . 93, 185
    state exemptions . . . 283–84
Wearing apparel . . . 94, 110
West Virginia exemptions . . . 93, 285–86
When attorney is needed . . . 19–23
Where bankruptcy cases are filed . . . 10–11, 91
"Wild card" federal exemption . . . 186
Willful acts
    failure to obey order of court . . . 26
    generally . . . 122
    malicious acts . . . 60–61
Wisconsin
    federal exemption . . . 93, 185
    state exemptions . . . 287–88

Y

About the Author

Judge William C. Hillman serves as a United States Bankruptcy Judge for the District of Massachusetts. Prior to becoming a bankruptcy judge, he practiced law with the firm of Strauss, Factor, Hillman & Lopes in Providence, Rhode Island, where, for more than 30 years, he represented debtors and creditors in bankruptcy proceedings. Judge Hillman obtained his preparatory education at the University of Chicago and Northwestern University, and J.D. (cum laude) and LL.M. degrees from Boston University. He has written extensively, particularly in the areas of secured transactions and creditors' rights, and has been a member of numerous professional and public boards and commissions, including the National Conference of Commissioners on Uniform State Laws.